PAPER PIECED STAINED GLASS

Garden Stars

LIZ SCHWARTZ & STEPHEN SEIFERT

Zippy Designs Publishing Inc. ❧ *Home of The Foundation Piecer* ❧ *Newport, Virginia*

To see a world in a grain of sand and a heaven in a wild flower:
hold infinity in the palm of your hand and eternity in an hour.

—*William Blake*

Dedication

The dazzling designs created by the interplay of light and color have inspired artists for centuries. We dedicate this book to all of the many artists who have helped to bring the art of stained glass into the forefront of our culture. Without dedication to their craft, we would not be able to enjoy their magnificent creations today and continue to derive inspiration and pleasure from their works.

Acknowledgements

We would like to thank all of the great people in our lives who have helped us; we owe you our deepest gratitude. We would especially like to thank our loyal quilting friends for their continued encouragement and support; without you we would never have come this far.

Special thanks are in order for Ted Schwartz who has spent many of his days with Sebastian, showing him the wonders that nature has to offer.

To Robin Hypes, thank you for all of your effort in testing and stitching the patterns used in this book. You truly are a joy to work with.

Paper Pieced Stained Glass Garden Stars
Copyright © 2001 Liz Schwartz and Stephen Seifert. All rights reserved.

ISBN I-891497-05-7

Printed in Korea
06 05 04 03 02   6 5 4 3 2

Credits

Book Designer ....Liz Schwartz
Design Coordinator.............................Stephen Seifert
Garden Consultant ....Ted Schwartz
Quilting Assistant ....Robin Southern-Hypes

The information in this book is presented in good faith, but no warranty is given nor results guaranteed. Since Zippy Designs Publishing Inc. has no control over the choice of materials or procedures, the company assumes no responsibility for the use of this information.

Zippy Designs Publishing Inc.
RR I Box 187M
Newport, VA 24128
www.zippydesigns.com

Contents

Introduction

The dazzling bejeweled designs created by light beaming through vibrantly colored panes of glass has mesmerized artists for centuries. From the breathtaking vignettes of religious icons, the stunning Rose window in Chartres cathedral, to the sumptuous favrile vases created by Louis Comfort Tiffany over a century ago, the magic of beautifully colored glass continues to captivate and inspire artists in all media.

Quilters seem to have a special passion for color and texture, which makes the union of stained glass patterns and quilting a natural. The bold geometric shapes and gracefully curving lines are especially well suited to the precision offered by the foundation piecing technique. Stained glass quilts can be created quickly, easily, and accurately using paper piecing without the use of fusible bias tape or time consuming appliqué.

In much the same way that stained glass artistry has inspired artists, gardens have also been an uplifting source for design and color ideas. The delicate and colorful blooms offer an infinite number of possibilities to explore.

Building on the continued success of both the *Stained Glass Series* quilt (shown at right) originally featured in *The Foundation Piecer* and later in the best selling *Foundation Pieced Stained Glass Quilts,* this book takes the art of stained glass quilting ever further.

Here we present a collection of 48 new blocks inspired by garden flowers. In studying the symmetry of flowers, we found that the block units could be combined in such a way that produced a star, and with that *Garden Stars* began to evolve.

We have included a variety of both representational and abstract floral patterns. The stained glass effect and subtlety of the star designs in each block make this a truly stunning addition to our stained glass block collection.

When designing each of the blocks, we tried to capture some essential element of the flower for which it is named. While some are easy to see, others are more abstract and can lend themselves to a variety of similar flowers. When stitching the blocks, we chose floral prints that were representational of the flower, to carry the theme through the block. While it is not necessary to match the flowers in the fabric to each of the blocks, we did so where possible.

It is our hope that you will use these designs as a starting point in creating your own quilts. Individual blocks can be combined to make table runners, tote-bags, vests, small wall hangings, bed quilts, or used in block exchanges. These new blocks may be combined with the 36 originally presented in *Foundation Pieced Stained Glass Quilts* for even more design possibilities.

Whether you wish to continue to expand your repertoire of blocks, or create your own vision of the garden, we are sure that you will enjoy stitching this exciting new collection of stained glass quilting blocks.

We immensely enjoy seeing all of your creations and hearing of the pleasure that you have had stitching the original stained glass patterns, and the joy that your quilts have given to those who have been the privileged recipients of such wondrous gifts. It is our sincere wish that these designs continue to be made into quilts that will be cherished for generations and bring you hours of pleasure in the making.

Liz Schwartz & Stephen Seifert
February 2001
Newport, Virginia

The Stained Glass series quilt as it appeared in The Foundation Piecer *and* Foundation Pieced Stained Glass Quilts

Paper Piecing Basics

Fabric Selection

While we prefer to use mainly 100% cotton fabrics in our quilts, foundation piecing lends itself to using a variety of different materials. The foundation helps to stabilize slippery fabrics and makes sewing much easier. You can combine different types of fabric within a block to create interesting effects.

The fabrics that you choose for your quilt brings the design to life. While fabric and color selection are largely a matter of personal preference, we like to follow a few simple guidelines to help make the process easier. Of course, these are only suggestions so feel free to exercise your creative spirit in developing your own style.

Feature Fabric | Start by first selecting a focal print that reflects the theme of the block, or a piece of fabric that inspires you. The feature fabric should be a high contrast medium- to large-scale print that has multiple colors and textures. We chose floral prints for most of the blocks in this book to echo the garden theme and help to carry the floral motif through each of the blocks.

The role of the feature fabric is to set the tone for the block and help guide you when selecting coordinating colors for the remaining fabrics.

Coordinates | With the feature fabric taking center stage, the role of the coordinating fabrics is to act as the supporting cast. Choose colors that are similar to those in the main print that you want to emphasize, using smaller amounts of contrasting colors for highlights. It is not necessary for the coordinates to be exact color matches, often adding a color that does not seem to fit may add sparkle to the design.

Coordinates are typically low contrast, small-scale prints with mainly monochromatic, or closely related color schemes, that tend to be muted and not very busy. Good examples of these fabrics are solids, tone-on-tone prints, hand-dyed fabrics, and textured prints.

The grouping above shows the feature fabric (bottom) and 3 coordinates (top). The coordinates help to emphasize the colors in the feature print and unify the overall color scheme of the block.

Mixing the Colors | After you have selected all of the fabrics, make several copies of the block foundation to audition color placement before you start sewing. Using colored pencils, shade each of the areas with the desired colors, or rough cut fabric swatches and glue them to the foundation. We like to place the feature fabric in the largest area, but it can be placed anywhere you like. Experiment with different positions, and consider all of the design possibilities. It is also fun to select a repeating motif from the fabric and place it in a very specific spot in the block (see the examples below).

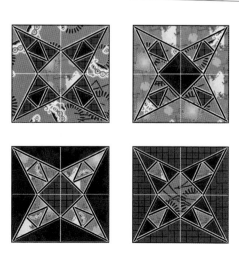

Several options for color placement in the *Delphinium Star* block. Notice how rearranging the colors gives the block an entirely different look. In the block on the lower left hand side, a butterfly motif was centered in piece 1 of each foundation.

Supplies

- Wooden seam pressing bar
- Add-A-Quarter template ruler
- Sewing machine
- Iron and ironing board
- Flannel press cloth
- Size 90/14 sewing machine needles
- Sewing thread
- Rotary cutter and mat
- Rotary rulers: 6" × 24" and 12½" × 12½"
- Vinyl-coated paper clips
- Sewing pins
- Tweezers (for removing paper)

Foundation Materials

Fabric | When you want your foundation to be permanent, you can transfer it to fabric by tracing or using an iron-transfer fabric pen. This foundation will add stability to the finished piece. The extra layer may make hand quilting more difficult. Suitable fabrics include prewashed muslin, polyester-cotton blends, and non-woven interfacing.

Paper | Just about any type of paper will make a suitable foundation. It is advisable to test the paper first to make sure that it handles well and does not fall out prematurely or shrink when ironed. We like Easy Piece foundation paper; it is translucent and easy to remove from the finished project. Other suitable papers include typing paper, onion skin, vellum, copy paper, tracing paper, parchment, and freezer paper.

Preparing the Foundations

To use the patterns presented in this book, they must first be duplicated so that they can be stitched. There are many methods that can be used to reproduce the foundations: needlepunching, photocopying, tracing, and scanning.

Needlepunching | This technique works best when many copies of the same block are needed; it is not especially suited to reproducing foundations for pictorial quilts. First, trace the pattern onto a piece of tracing paper. Layer the traced pattern with up to ten sheets of paper. Then, with an unthreaded sewing machine, sew along the lines.

Photocopying | Photocopying is the fastest and easiest way to make foundations for your project. For best results, we recommend that you test the accuracy of the machine before making all of your copies for the entire project. To do this, make a copy of the pattern on the machine. Place the copy over the original and hold it up to a light source. Look to see how closely the original matches the copy. If the copy is significantly different, choose another machine. To minimize distortion when copying, use the same machine and make all of the copies needed for the project at the same time.

Tracing | Although time consuming, tracing is an easy and accurate way to make copies that can be used with both fabric and paper foundations. Use a very fine mechanical pencil to carefully trace over the marked patterns lines. Work slowly and carefully to assure that the units will fit together properly when they are joined.

Scanning | When laying the foundation master on the scanner bed, make sure that there are no stray objects or wrinkles which might cause gaps in the final scan. Choose a moderately high resolution— 150 to 200 dpi to derive the most detail without overloading the computer with more information than is necessary. Once the image is scanned, you can print out as many copies as you like without going to the copy shop or spending the time to trace each foundation by hand.

After you have made all of the necessary foundations for the project, trim them out leaving about a ¼" seam allowance around the dashed lines. To prepare the foundations for stitching, mark the colors in the spaces.

When cutting fabric strips, first locate the largest piece where the fabric will be used. Then, cut the widest strips first to avoid running short on fabric.

Cutting Fabric Pieces

Rather than cutting out the shape of the piece, as you would for traditional patchwork, we cut fabric strips of varying widths and use them to piece the foundation sections. Using these strips helps to minimize fabric waste and keeps things organized.

1 Starting with piece 1, measure the height and width of the area by placing a rotary ruler over the section covered by the piece. Add at least a ½" seam allowance around each of the sides; the extra fabric will help to ensure that the fabric patch covers the area if it shifts during sewing.

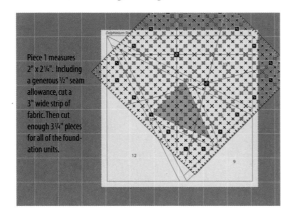

Piece 1 measures 2" x 2¼". Including a generous ½" seam allowance, cut a 3" wide strip of fabric. Then cut enough 3¼" pieces for all of the foundation units.

2 Cut a strip of fabric to the width of the measurement. Then cut a fabric patch from the strip to the length of the piece. Continue cutting pieces from the strip for all of the foundation sections.

3 To measure for the next piece, lay the edge of the ruler along the seam line between pieces 1 and 2, so that it entirely covers piece 2. Look to see how large the piece is including the seam allowance. Cut a strip of fabric to the width of the measurement, then use the strip to cut the pieces needed.

To create an interesting kaleidoscope effect, use the technique for directional fabrics. Instead of placing the piece on the straight of grain, be sure to center the design motif in the piece as you want it to appear when finished. Then, cut it as you would a directional fabric.

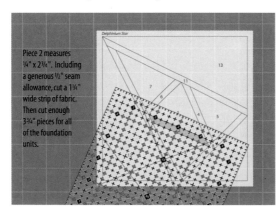

Piece 2 measures ¼" x 2¾". Including a generous ½" seam allowance, cut a 1¼" wide strip of fabric. Then cut enough 3¾" pieces for all of the foundation units.

4 Repeat the process described above to cut fabric pieces for all of the remaining sections.

Cutting Directional Fabrics

Directional prints such as stripes and plaids may be used successfully in foundation piecing but look best when cut and pieced so that they are placed on the straight of grain.

1 Cut a piece of fabric that covers the entire area plus seam allowances (in the example below, the directional fabric will be used in piece 3). When cutting the fabric, place it so that the straight of grain is parallel to the edges of the foundation, and the print is positioned as it will be in the finished block. Place the foundation, with the printed side up, on top of the wrong side of the directional fabric. Center the piece in the area and check to see that it covers the entire area including a generous ½" seam allowance around all sides of the piece.

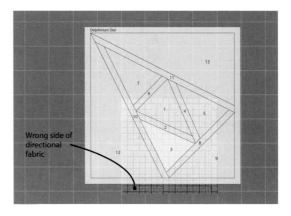

Wrong side of directional fabric

2 Place the edge of an index card on the line between the previous piece and the section in which the fabric will be used (in the example below, the card was placed on the line between pieces 2 and 3). Crease the foundation along the sewing line and fold it down over the index card. Place an Add-A-Quarter ruler on top of the folded foundation and card, pushing the ¼" lip up against the fold.

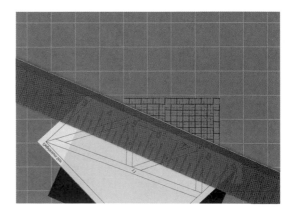

3 | Using a rotary cutter, trim away the excess material. Using the cut piece as a template, trim enough pieces of fabric for the remaining foundation sections. Repeat this process for all of the areas in which the directional fabric will be used.

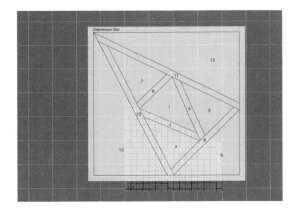

Grain

When cutting fabric and piecing blocks, we do not usually concern ourselves with the grain of the fabric; it is possible to cut and position each piece so that it is on the straight of grain, as described with directional fabrics. We almost always use fabric strips unless we are working with a directional print, such as a check or stripe, that will look awkward if it is not positioned on the straight of grain.

As long as your finished quilt is bordered by fabric that is cut from the straight of grain, you should not encounter any problems using this approach. We also highly recommend that you baste each of your finished sections within the ¼" seam allowance to prevent any distortion or stretching of the fabric when you are assembling the sections. When basting the foundations, use a very small stitch. The stitches do not need to be removed and will help to stabilize the edges and prevent them from fraying. After the quilt top has been completed, remove the paper. The tiny stitches allow the paper to be easily torn away.

Foundation Piecing Primer

Sewing the Foundation Units

After the pieces have been cut and the foundations are prepared, it is time to start sewing. The side of the foundation that is marked with the pattern lines and numbers is what you will be looking at when you are stitching the units; the fabrics will be placed on the unmarked (blank) side of the paper.

1 | Place your first fabric piece right side up on the wrong (unprinted) side of the foundation. Holding the unit up to a light source (printed side of the foundation facing you), position the first piece of fabric. Make sure that the fabric covers the entire area including a ¼" seam allowance. Pin in place, or use a dab of glue from a glue stick.

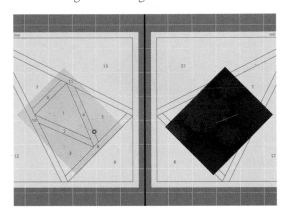

2 | Align a post card along the sewing line between pieces 1 and 2. Crease the paper and fold it over the postcard to reveal the excess fabric below.

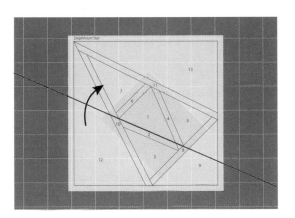

3 | Place an Add-A-Quarter ruler on the crease and push the ¼" lip up against the fold. Using a rotary cutter, trim the excess fabric leaving a ¼" seam allowance.

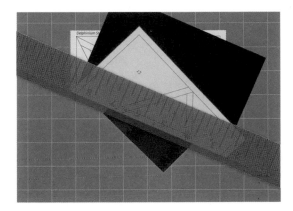

Before you begin sewing, replace your needle with a size 90/14 and reduce your stitch length to 15–20 per inch.

To protect your ironing board from the ink on the foundations, place a flannel press cloth on top of the surface to absorb the ink.

4 | Align the next fabric patch, right side down, along the pre-trimmed edge. Looking through the paper from the printed side, check to see that the piece of fabric being added extends beyond the stitching line.

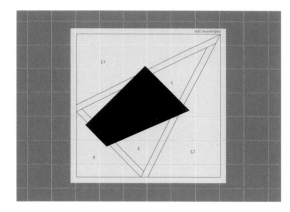

When adding a piece which forms an acute angle with the previous piece, extend your line of stitching at least ½" past the printed sewing line so that you will have enough fabric to maintain a ¼" seam allowance.

5 | Flip the foundation (with the fabrics in place) to the printed side and sew on the line between the first and second pieces. Extend your line of stitching at least ¼" before and after the printed line (this helps prevent the seams from ripping out).

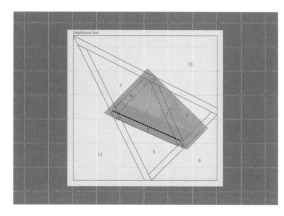

6 | Place the foundation, with the printed side down, on a flannel press cloth. Fold the fabric into place and press it with an iron. Holding the fabric firmly, press the seam with a wooden seam pressing bar to flatten the seam.

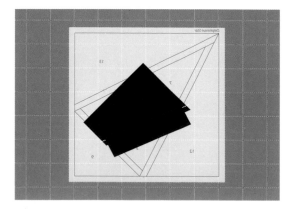

7 | Place the postcard on the next sewing line (between pieces 2 and 3) and fold the paper over the postcard. If previous stitching prevents you from folding the foundation, carefully tear the paper away from those stitches so it folds easily. Place the Add-A-Quarter ruler on the fold, and trim away the excess material, leaving a ¼" seam allowance.

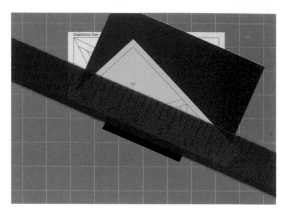

8 | With right sides together, place the next piece of fabric on the blank (fabric) side of the foundation and align it with the pre-trimmed edge. Holding the unit up to a light source, check to see if the piece extends at least ¼" past the the sewing line.

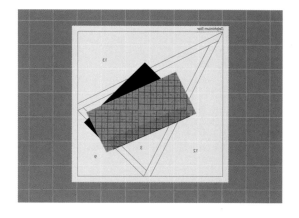

9 | Flip the unit to the printed side and sew on the line between pieces 2 and 3. Continue pressing, trimming, and adding pieces until completed.

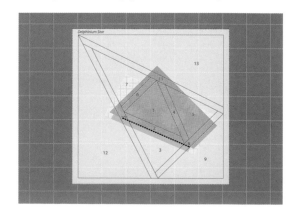

10 | Using a very small stitch, baste around the entire foundation within the ¼" seam allowance. Be careful that the basting does not extend into the visible areas of the section (past the solid line).

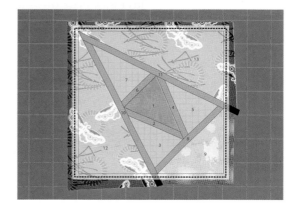

11 | Trim the foundation along the outer (dashed) line, removing the excess fabric and paper from the section. Do not remove the paper from the blocks yet, as it helps to stabilize the fabric and aids in assembling the block.

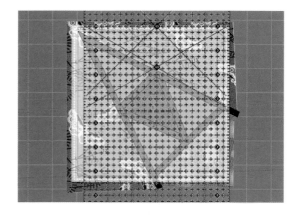

Assembling the Block

12 | With the printed side facing you, arrange all of the units as shown in the **Assembly Diagram.** Turn the units to the fabric side and check to see if any mistakes were made while sewing the units.

13 | Identify several key points (such as corners, center seams, and obvious match points) and place pins through them so that the pin passes perpendicularly through the sewing (solid) lines on both foundations. When the sections are aligned, fasten them together using several vinyl-coated paper clips.

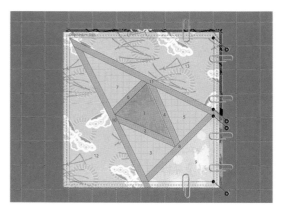

14 | After the paper clips are set, remove all of the pins. Sew the units together, removing the paper clips as you sew. Be careful not to sew over the paper clips as they can damage your needle and cause the layers to shift.

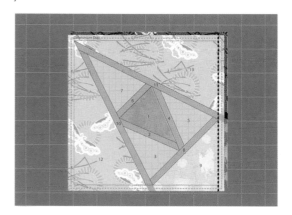

15 | Carefully remove the paper only from the seam allowance area and press the seam open. Sew the remaining units together and join the halves to make the block.

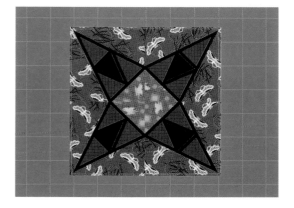

If you make a mistake and need to replace a piece of fabric, gently remove the stitches with a seam ripper; then remove the piece of fabric and resew the seam. A ripped foundation can easily be repaired with a little transparent tape. However, if you sew over the tape it leaves a sticky residue on the needle.

The Blocks

Using the Patterns

With each block design you will find: a color photo of the finished piece, a photo of 4 blocks grouped together, special assembly instructions and diagram, and a set of full-sized foundation masters to complete a 12" finished block.

Assembly Diagram | A visual map to block construction, the **Assembly Diagram** shows how the sections fit together to make the design. It is important to note that the **Assembly Diagram** shows the foundations from the printed side; the fabric side will be the mirror image of what is shown. Even though it may seem intuitive to flip the foundations over and look at the fabric side, all of the assembly steps are best done looking only at the printed side of the foundation.

Foundations | The printed side of the foundation is the mirror image, or reverse, of the finished block (fabric side). Looking through the unprinted (blank) side of the paper will help to visualize the finished block. Since you are sewing on the back of the design, the finished block will be the reverse of both the foundation pattern and the **Assembly Diagram.** To avoid confusion when making the sections, look at the foundation from the unprinted side when envisioning fabric placement. The black leading areas are shaded in gray to aid in unit construction.

Changing the Finished Size | When making copies of your foundations, it is easy to change the finished size using a copy machine. Use the following chart to determine the percentage to enlarge or reduce the block foundations.

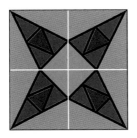

Assembly Diagram for the *Delphinium Star* block (left) and photo (right). Both of these appear similar as the foundation pattern is perfectly symmetrical. The image (foundation) and its reverse (finished block) are identical.

Assembly Diagram for the *Clematis Star* block (left) and photo (right). Since this design is asymmetrical, the pinwheels appear to spin in the opposite direction in the finished block (right).

To assemble blocks that need multiple units for each block quarter, locate the lowercase letters in the seam allowances of the sections. Starting with *a* to *a*, match the lowercase letters and join the units alphabetically.

Block Reduction and Enlargement Chart	
Desired Block Finished Size	**Enlargement or Reduction (% of original)**
18"	150%
17"	142%
16"	133%
15"	125%
14"	117%
13"	108%
12"	100% †
11"	92%
10"	83%
9"	75%
8"	67%
7"	58%
6"	50%

† Original Size
Note that reducing and enlarging the size of the finished block also changes the thickness of the leading.

African Violet Star

Amaryllis Star

Bleeding Heart Star

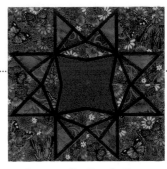

Butterfly Bush Star

Camellia Star

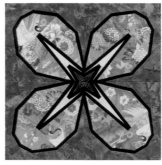

Cherry Blossom Star

Clematis Star

Cosmos Star

Crabapple Star

Crocus Star

Daffodil Star

Dahlia Star

Daisy Star

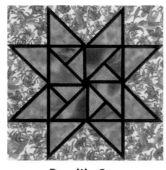

Daylily Star

Delphinium Star

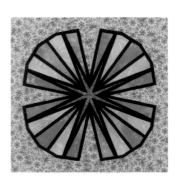

Dianthus Star

Freesia Star

Hibiscus Star

Hollyhock Star

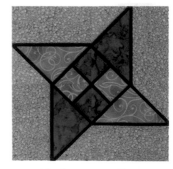

Hydrangea Star

Japanese Iris Star

Lady's Slipper Star

Larkspur Star

Lavender Star

Lilac Star

Lily-of-the-Valley Star

Lupine Star

Magnolia Star

Mistletoe Star

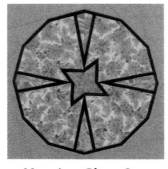

Morning Glory Star

Nasturtium Star

Petunia Star

Plum Blossom Star

Poinsettia Star

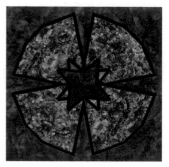

Poppy Star

Prickly Pear Star

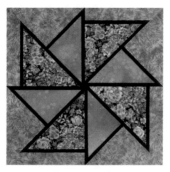

Primrose Star

Queen Anne's Lace Star

Rhododendron Star

Saguaro Star

Strawflower Star

Sunflower Star

Toad Lily Star

Tulip Star

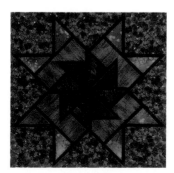

Viola Star

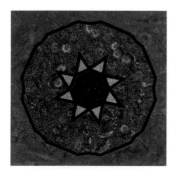

Wild Rose Star

Wisteria Star

Zinnia Star

African Violet Star

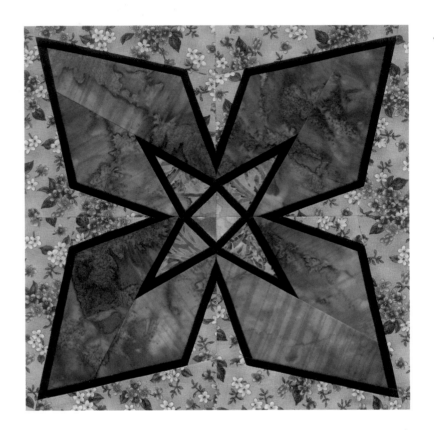

African violets are highly popular and familiar flowering house-plants. Many people, remembering their mother's and grandmother's plants, assume that all african violets have deep blue flowers and plain green leaves. Though this was true of the original plants discovered in the forest understory of Kenya and Tanzania, mutations and the enthusiastic work of breeders, have developed modern african violets with many flower colors. Today, it is common to see flowers in colors including many shades of white, blue, purple, red, pink, lavender, and coral.

Assembly

Make 4 of the foundation unit. Stitch the quarters together to make the block.

Yardage Requirements (for one block)

⅛ yd. black (leading)
⅛ yd. each light purple and yellow
¼ yd. each green floral (background) and dark purple

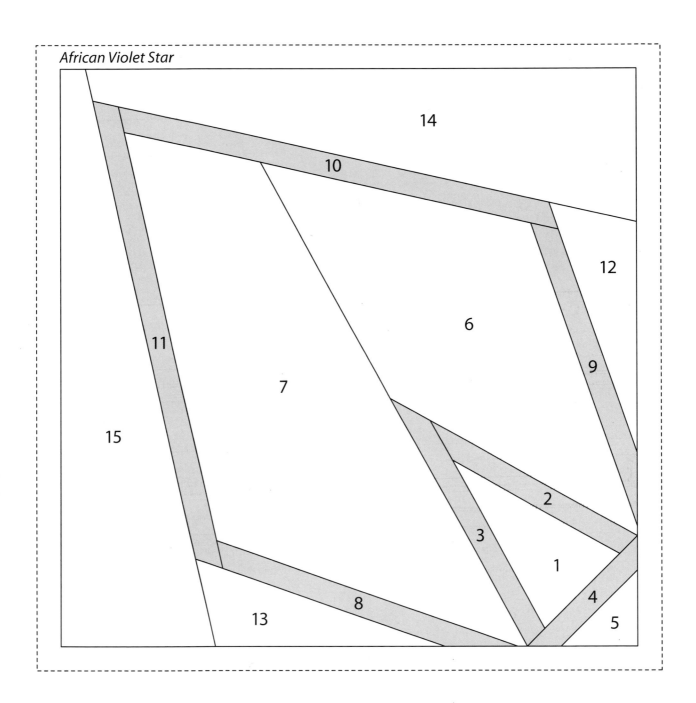

African Violet Star

Amaryllis Star

The popular winter flowering amaryllis, widely cultivated in pots for its winter bloom, is botanically classified under the genus Hippeastrum. Originally from South America, this large bulb is widely available in stores for fall and winter indoor planting. A wonderful plant for those of us who are impatient, its bloom stalk grows so rapidly that daily growth can be seen. Today the center for amaryllis production is in the Netherlands where single and double pink, white, and even green flowers have joined the lovely dark reds, coming into bloom just in time for Christmas.

Assembly

Make 4 each of foundation units A–C. Matching the lowercase letters in the seam allowances, stitch the units together alphabetically. Join the quarters.

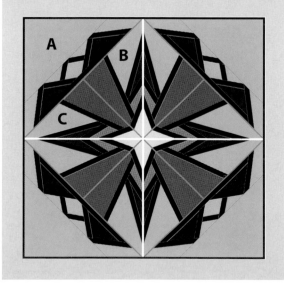

Yardage Requirements (for one block)

¼ yd. black (leading)
⅛ yd. each light pink, medium pink, dark pink, light green, dark green, and cream.
¼ yd. light blue floral (background)

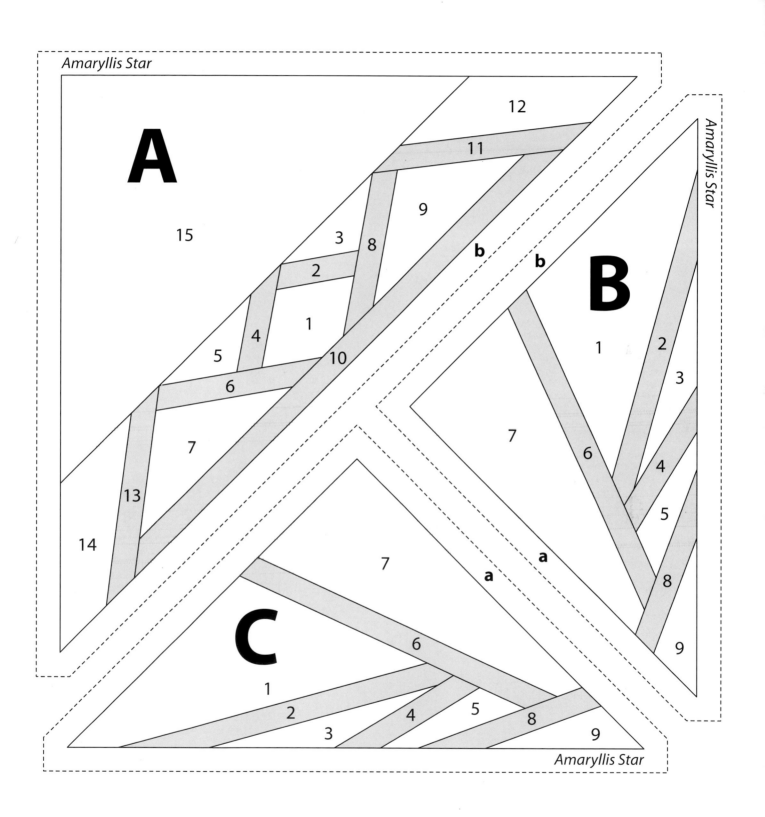

Amaryllis Star

A

B

C

Amaryllis Star

Amaryllis Star

Bleeding Heart Star

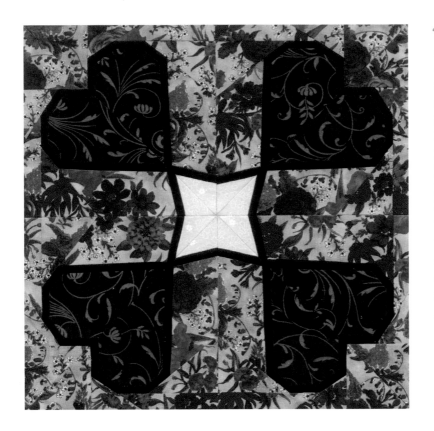

Bleeding hearts are a favorite choice for the woodland garden, often planted with spring blooming bulbs. They require moist soil and at least partial shade. The ferny divided foliage of the bleeding heart forms a beautiful loose mound. Pink and white locket shaped flowers hang from lovely arched stems, staying in bloom for about 6 weeks. As warmer weather approaches, they tend to go dormant. There are also bleeding hearts that grow and bloom throughout the summer. We enjoy both types in our garden. Once established, bleeding hearts are long-lived plants that can become garden favorites over the years.

Assembly

Make 4 of foundation units A and B. Join the triangles to make a total of 4 squares. Sew the quarters together to make the block.

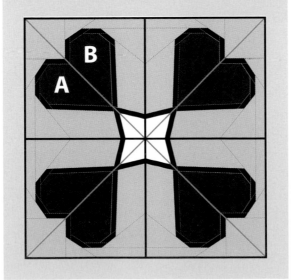

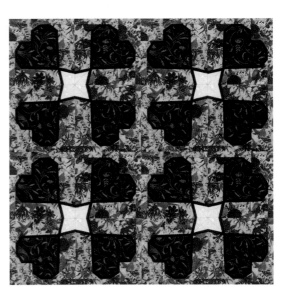

Yardage Requirements (for one block)

⅛ yd. black (leading)
⅛ yd. each red and white
¼ yd. tan floral (background)

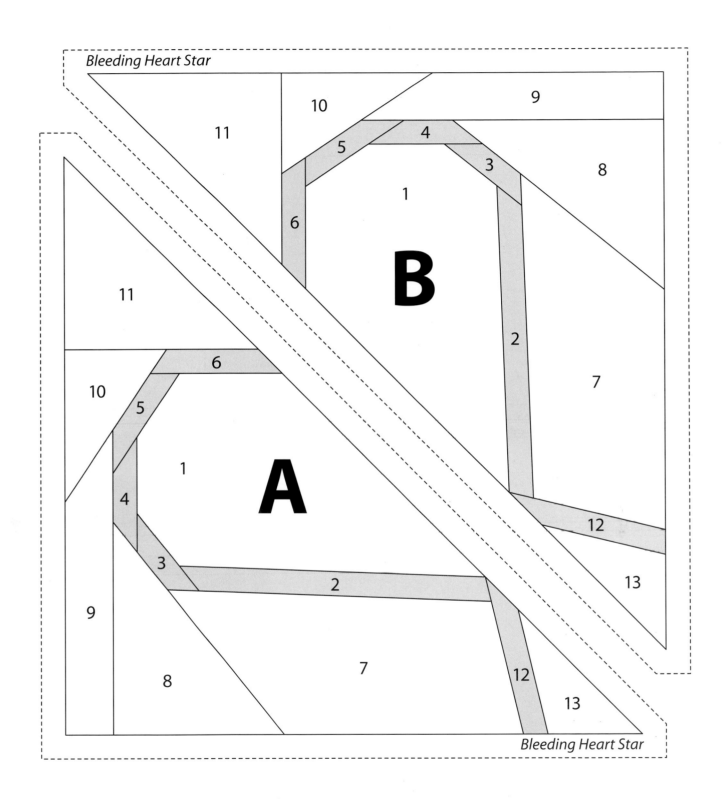

Bleeding Heart Star

Bleeding Heart Star

Butterfly Bush Star

The Buddleia, or butterfly bush, is a popular flowering shrub that no garden should be without. Easily transplanted, almost weed-like in its ability to survive, it is very easy to root from summer cuttings. Butterfly bushes are best pruned down to the ground every spring since they can grow up to 10 feet in a growing season. The fragrant flowers can attract a large number of butterflies and bees. Usually seen in lavender, blue, deep purple, pink, and white, now even yellow varieties are available. The number of cultivars and colors of this amazingly easy to grow shrub continue to grow, attesting to its universal popularity.

Assembly

Make 4 of foundation units A and B. Join the triangles to make a total of 4 squares. Sew the quarters together to make the block.

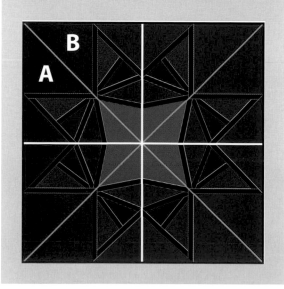

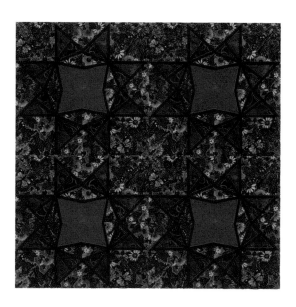

Yardage Requirements (for one block)

⅛ yd. black (leading)
⅛ yd. each orange, yellow, and purple
¼ yd. blue floral (background)

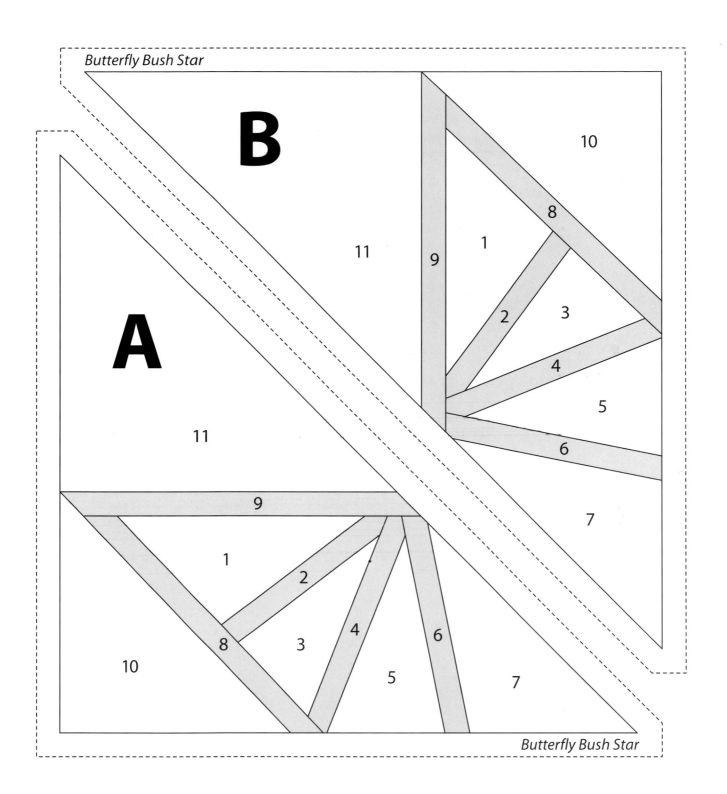

Butterfly Bush Star

B

A

Camellia Star

Living in the mountains of Southwest Virginia, Camellia japonica planted in the garden rarely survive our winters. Even in a greenhouse, they prefer cool conditions, making it impossible for them to share space with warm loving plants. Of course, in the Deep South they are glorious, unfurling their fragile waxen blossoms in fall through early spring, at a time when there are few other flowers in bloom. A large blooming shrub covered with hundreds of rose-like blooms and shiny leathery leaves is really a joy to behold, which for some of us almost makes up for the flower's lack of fragrance.

Assembly

Make 4 of the foundation unit. Stitch the quarters together to make the block.

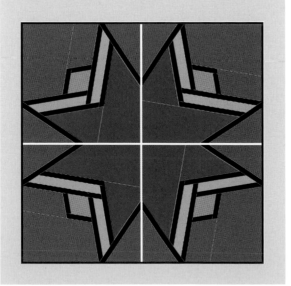

Yardage Requirements (for one block)

⅛ yd. black (leading)
⅛ yd. each green, light peach, and blue floral*
¼ yd. each medium peach (background)

*extra material may be needed to center floral motifs as shown in photos

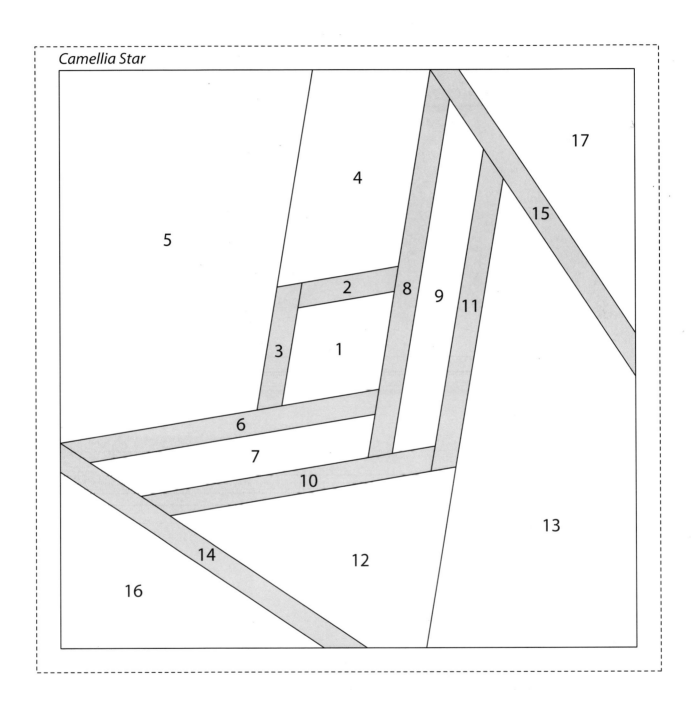

Camellia Star

Cherry Blossom Star

For us, spring truly arrives in April when our Japanese cherry tree covers itself with delicate blossoms. Serenity lies at the heart of every Japanese garden. As an artistic expression of the essence of nature, Japanese gardens draw upon the world's tranquil beauty to create an oasis for meditation and contemplation in a society, which for many is becoming somewhat overwhelming. Our rendition of the cherry blossom attempts to capture the feeling of serenity in fabric and thread. Spending time on our quilt projects gives us an opportunity for self renewal and peaceful thought.

Assembly

Make 4 of the foundation unit. Stitch the quarters together to make the block.

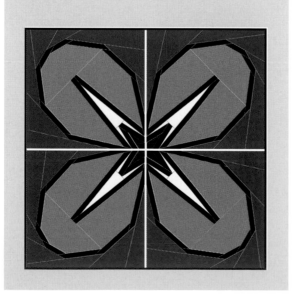

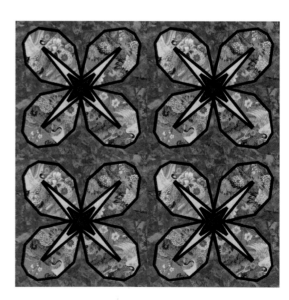

Yardage Requirements (for one block)

¼ yd. black (leading)
⅛ yd. each orange and white
¼ yd. each blue (background) and tan floral*

*extra material may be needed to center floral motifs as shown in photos

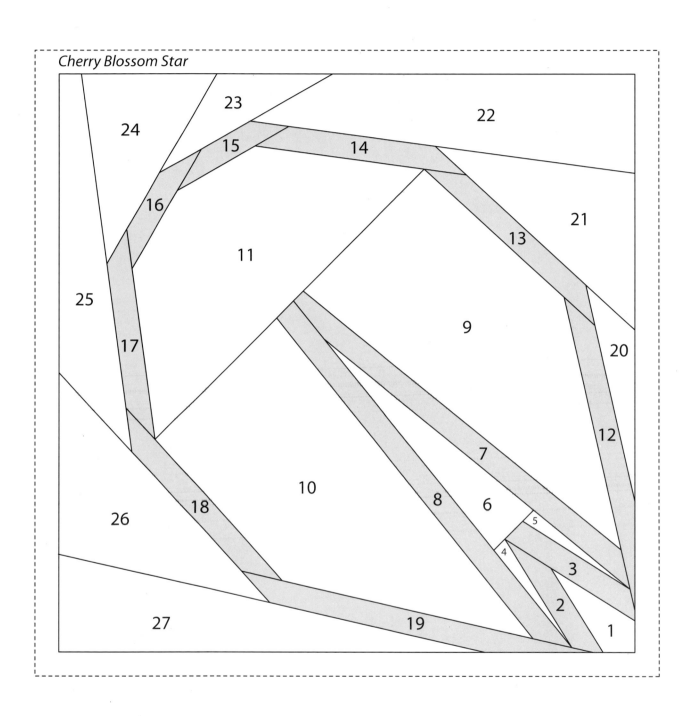

Cherry Blossom Star

Clematis Star

Considered by many to be the finest flowering vine, clematis can completely cover its leaves with sensational blooms. They can be trained to grow on arbors and trellises, as well as walls and fences. The vines can also be found scrambling across the ground hiding stumps, or as we like to grow them, up through taller trees and shrubs where they happily bloom and thrive. Available in almost all colors of the rainbow, it is hard to imagine a plant that grows only a few inches the first year can grow 8 to 10 feet the next. Our version of this perennial favorite reminds me of a late spring country garden complete with a trellis.

Assembly

Make 4 of the foundation unit. Stitch the quarters together to make the block.

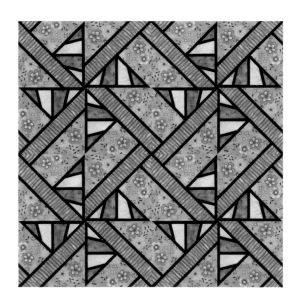

Yardage Requirements (for one block)

¼ yd. black (leading)
⅛ yd. light pink, dark pink and green stripe
¼ yd. blue floral (background)

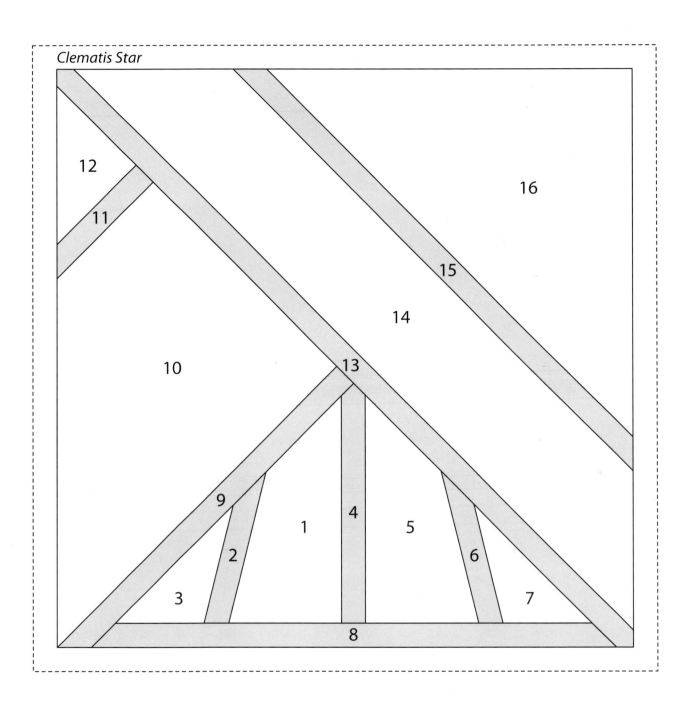

Clematis Star

Cosmos Star

Cosmos are so easy to grow that they seem to thrive on neglect. As a child, I remember they were one of the only things that grew from a packet of mixed seeds dumped on the ground and promptly forgotten about. Today in much the same way, they rapidly grow from seeds sown directly into the garden. Lovely satin like blooms in shades of pink or purple are my favorite, but they also come in white, red, candy stripe, and shades of yellow, gold, and orange. They are perfect for spur of the moment bouquets. In fact, the more you pick, the more they seem to bloom. If you are new to gardening or do not have a green thumb, try growing cosmos. I think you will be glad you did.

Assembly

Make 4 of foundation units A and B. Join the triangles to make a total of 4 squares. Sew the quarters together to make the block.

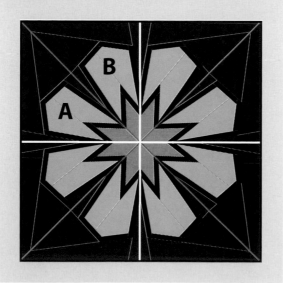

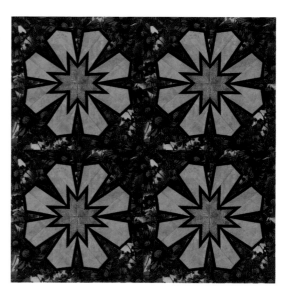

Yardage Requirements (for one block)

¼ yd. black (leading)
⅛ yd. each light pink and yellow
¼ yd. magenta floral (background)

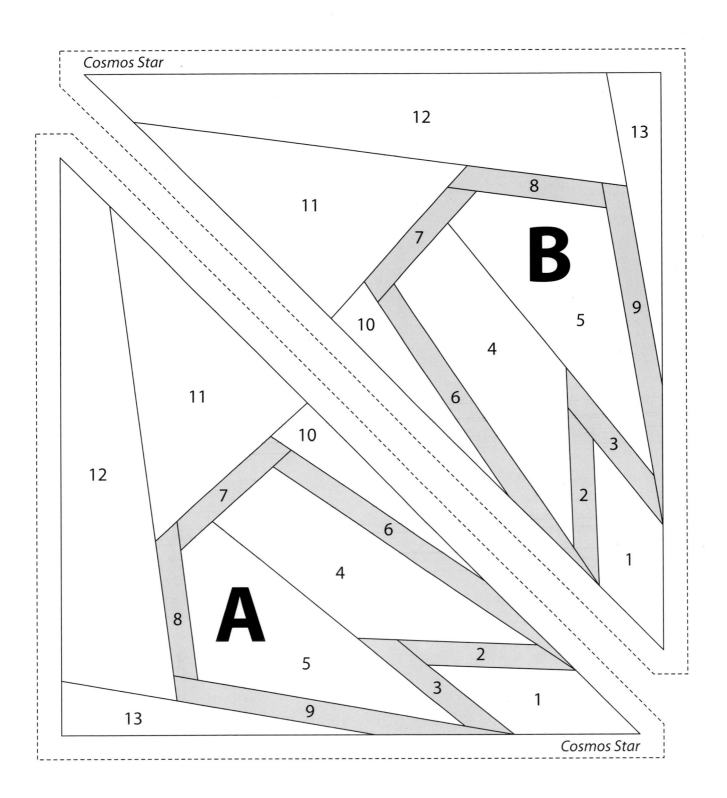

Cosmos Star

Cosmos Star

Crabapple Star

Flowering crabapples are among the most beautiful of all spring flowering trees and shrubs, outdoing even the more famous Japanese flowering cherries. Not only are they beautiful in bloom, they are attractive in fall when they produce a prolific crop of brightly colored fruit. The ornamental character of both the flowers and fruits gives flowering crabapples great value as a garden plant. We especially like the Dolgo crabapple, whose large fruit can be used to make wonderful sauces and jellies. As an alternative to a more traditional pink and white color scheme, we chose to celebrate autumn and the bounty of the crabapple crop in our version of this lovely block.

Assembly

Make 4 of foundation units A and B. Join the triangles to make a total of 4 squares. Sew the quarters together to make the block.

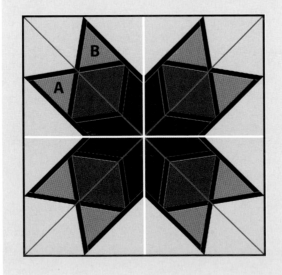

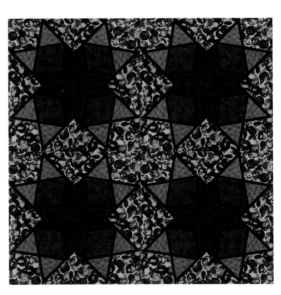

Yardage Requirements (for one block)

⅛ yd. black (leading)
⅛ yd. each red, green, and brown
¼ yd. tan fruit print (background)

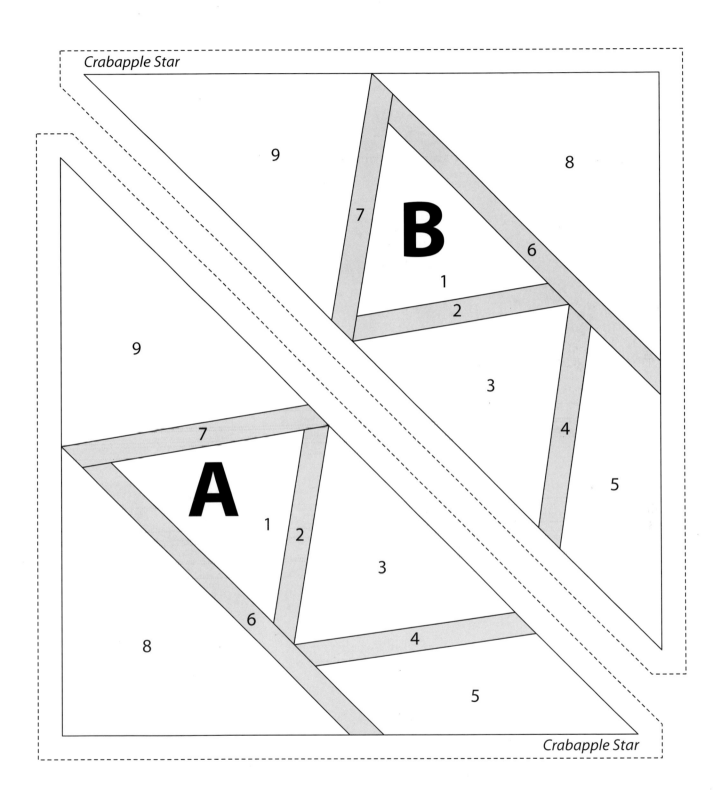

Crabapple Star

Crabapple Star

Crocus Star

Since ancient times, the crocus has been the symbol of life, beauty, and youth. It is impossible to dissociate the crocus from springtime, and in Northern Europe, it is rare to find a house without a pot of multi-colored crocuses. In the United States, the most widely available crocuses are the large flowering hybrids in shades of purple, blue, yellow, and white. However, not all crocuses bloom in the spring. For the ancients, Crocus sativus, with its large lilac-purple flowers and long conspicuous orange stigmata, from which saffron is obtained, was the most common form blooming in the fall.

Assembly

Make 4 of foundation units A and B. Join the triangles to make a total of 4 squares. Sew the quarters together to make the block.

Yardage Requirements (for one block)

¼ yd. black (leading)
⅛ yd. each light yellow and green
¼ yd. each teal (background) and pink floral*

*extra material may be needed to center floral motifs as shown in photos

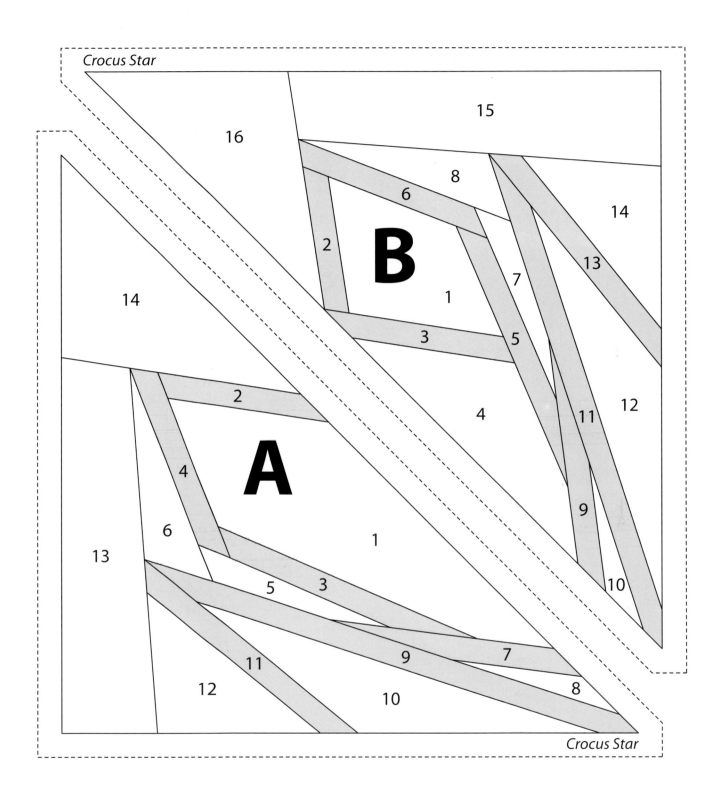

Crocus Star

Crocus Star

Daffodil Star

Heralding the arrival of spring, the big yellow trumpet daffodil is one of the best-loved and most recognizable flowers in the world. While all daffodils are narcissus, not all narcissus are daffodils. That is to say Narcissus refers to the genus name, which is comprised of 13 divisions ranging in size from tiny multi-colored forms a few inches high to the giant trumpet types. Colors vary from white and the palest of yellow to orange and even pink. If you select the right varieties, they will come back year after year. What a small investment to make for a lifetime of beauty.

Assembly

Make 4 of foundation units A and B. Join the triangles to make a total of 4 squares. Sew the quarters together to make the block.

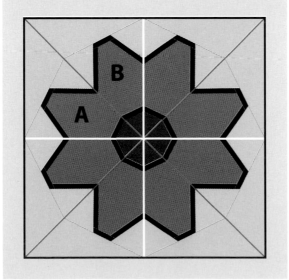

Yardage Requirements (for one block)

⅛ yd. black (leading)
⅛ yd. each dark yellow and floral print
¼ yd. light yellow (background)

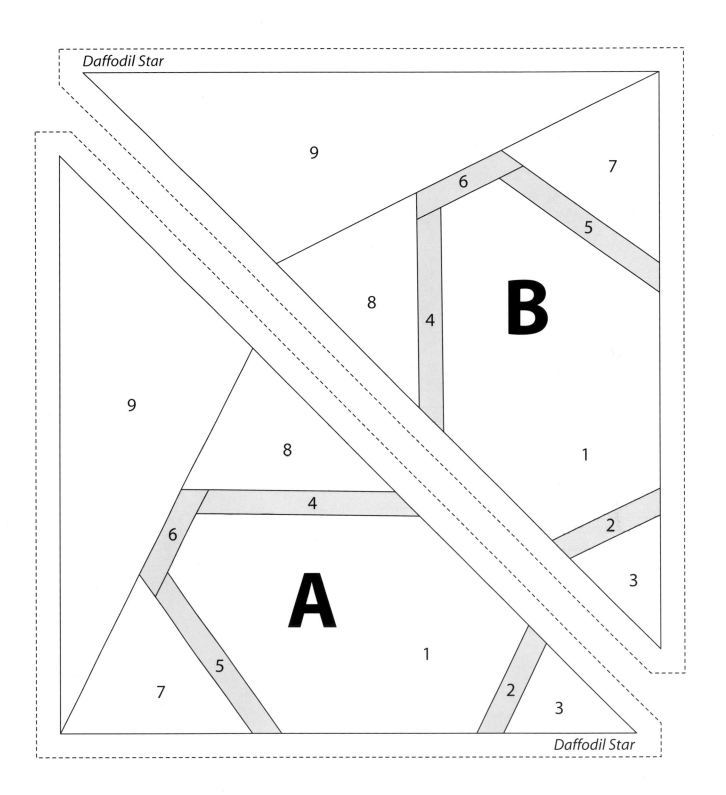

Daffodil Star

Daffodil Star

Dahlia Star

Dahlias are truly international plants, found in almost all parts of the world where there are gardens. The reason for this universal popularity is attributable to the fact that dahlias are so easy to grow, giving maximum results with minimal effort. They are healthy, vigorous plants, rarely ill or diseased, with frost as their only serious enemy. In autumn, with the arrival of cold weather, they collapse immediately and enter a dormant period during which they live on food and moisture stored in their tubers during the previous season. Dahlias are available from 18 inches tall to over 6 feet in a dazzling array of colors.

Assembly

Make 4 of the foundation unit. Stitch the quarters together to make the block.

Yardage Requirements (for one block)

⅛ yd. black (leading)
⅛ yd. each light magenta, dark magenta, yellow and rust/magenta floral
¼ yd. orange (background)

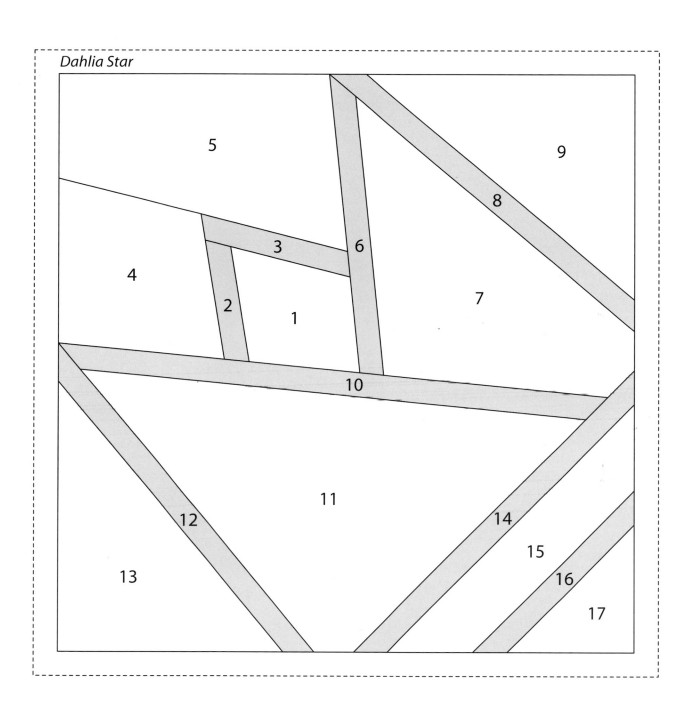

Dahlia Star

Daisy Star

When people talk about their favorite flowers, they will often say that it is the daisy. Many of us have childhood memories of white daisies with bright yellow centers. Others think of black and brown-eyed Susans blanketing the mid-summer landscape. Still others remember pink "daisies" which are actually mums. Ultimately, what we call a daisy refers to the general shape and structure of the flower. We chose to depict our daisy with golden yellow petals and a brown center, resembling the familiar rudbeckia. Many landscapers are now combining this daisy with ornamental grasses and other hardy plants to create a garden requiring low maintenance that has a casual natural beauty.

Assembly

Make 4 of foundation units A and B. Join the triangles to make a total of 4 squares. Sew the quarters together to make the block.

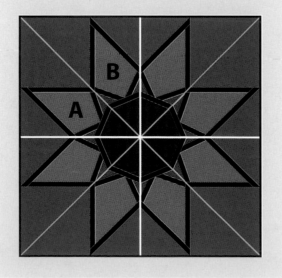

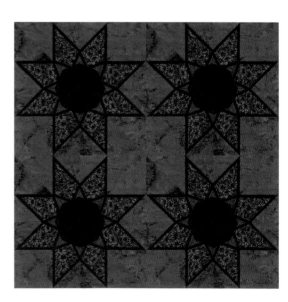

Yardage Requirements (for one block)

⅛ yd. black (leading)
⅛ yd. each yellow, brown, and floral print*
¼ yd. green (background)

*extra material may be needed to center floral motifs as shown in photos

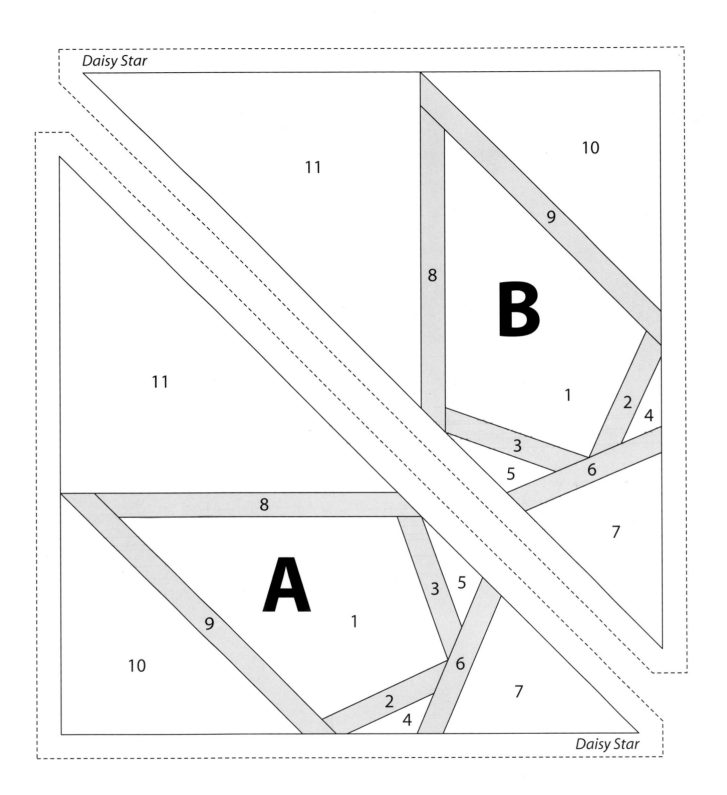

Daisy Star

Daisy Star

Daylily Star

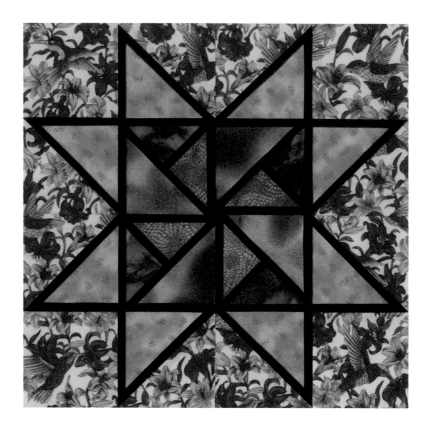

What would the perennial garden be without daylilies? They are so dependable, long blooming, and handsome that few plants are their equals. One of the most hybridized of all modern plants, there are thousands of named cultivars. Today, gardeners no longer have to settle for plain orange or yellow blooms, when luscious pinks and glorious crimsons are widely available. By doubling the number of chromosomes, breeders have created more vigorous plants with stocky stems and larger flowers. Surprisingly, Hemerocallis fulva, the tawny orange summer blooming daylily found growing wild in the United States, is actually native to China.

Assembly

Make 4 each of the foundation units A and B. Stitch the sections together to make 4 block quarters. Join the quarters.

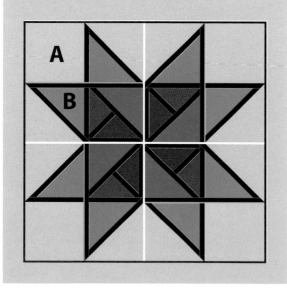

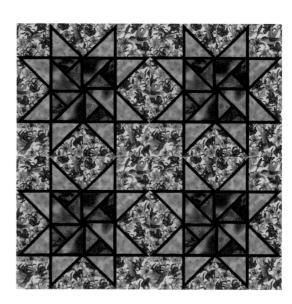

Yardage Requirements (for one block)

⅛ yd. black (leading)
⅛ yd. each blue, green, pink, and yellow
¼ yd. cream floral (background)

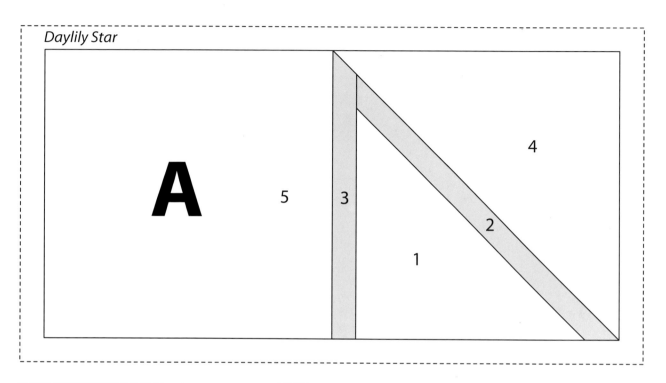

Daylily Star

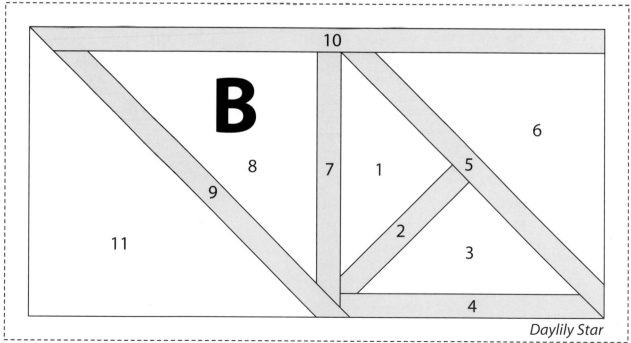

Delphinium Star

The delphinium is certainly one of the most beautiful cultivated flowers. It does particularly well in regions where the climate is cool and not too dry. In most of Great Britain, they grow gloriously tall and stately in rich blues, purples, and pinks. In the U.S. they thrive in areas of the New England coast and the Pacific Northwest. As with most flowers, hybridizers have been busy trying to develop varieties that are more tolerant of the warmer and drier weather that most gardeners have to contend with. There are several other perennial delphiniums available, all of which are worth growing, especially if you love hard to find blue flowers.

Assembly

Make 4 of the foundation unit. Stitch the quarters together to make the block.

Yardage Requirements (for one block)

⅛ yd. black (leading)
⅛ yd. each green, blue, and purple
¼ yd. blue floral (background)

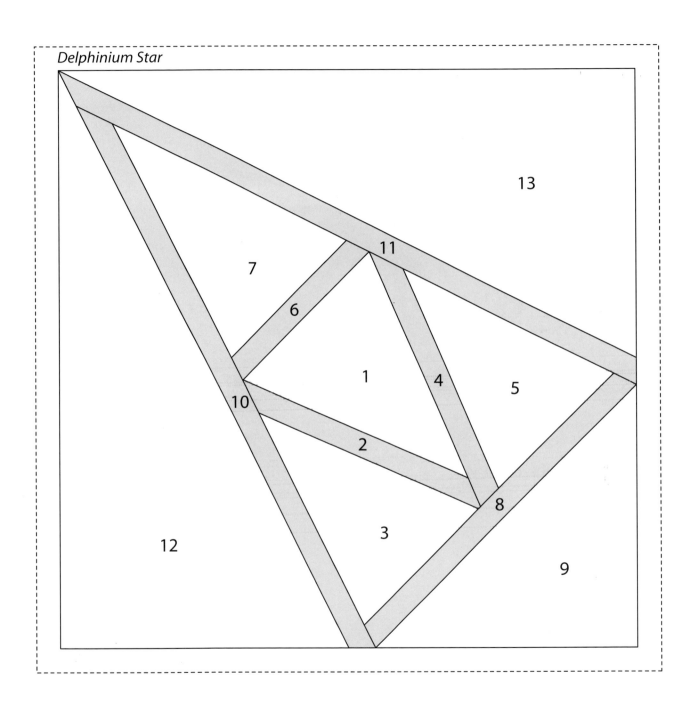

Delphinium Star

Dianthus Star

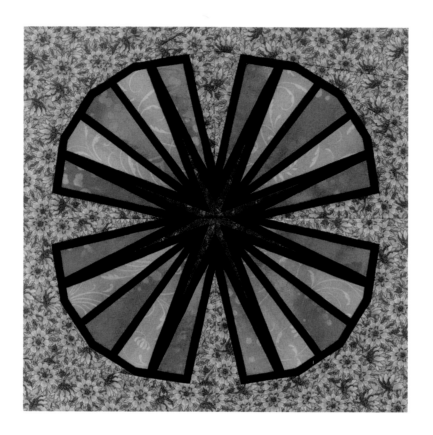

Dianthus is a large genus that is comprised of many forms of useful garden plants. What they all have in common is their lovely clove scent. Most are mound or matte forming plants that prefer dry sunny conditions. The blooms, which will cover the plants in springtime are fringed, or "pinked," hence the common name "pinks." Perhaps because these plants are usually found in shades of pink also helps to contribute to their name. We especially like the cultivar called Bath's Pink; it dependably comes back every year with almost no care. We use it as an edging plant along a natural stone wall where the pink flowers and gray-green leaves yields an outstanding color combination.

Assembly

Make 4 of the foundation unit. Stitch the quarters together to make the block.

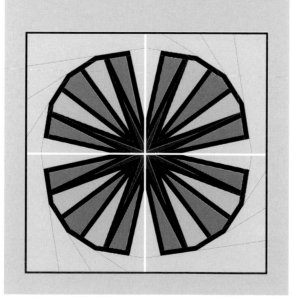

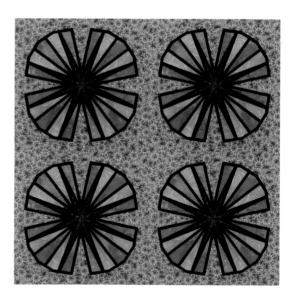

Yardage Requirements (for one block)

¼ yd. black (leading)
⅛ yd. each green, light pink, and medium pink
¼ yd. tan floral (background)

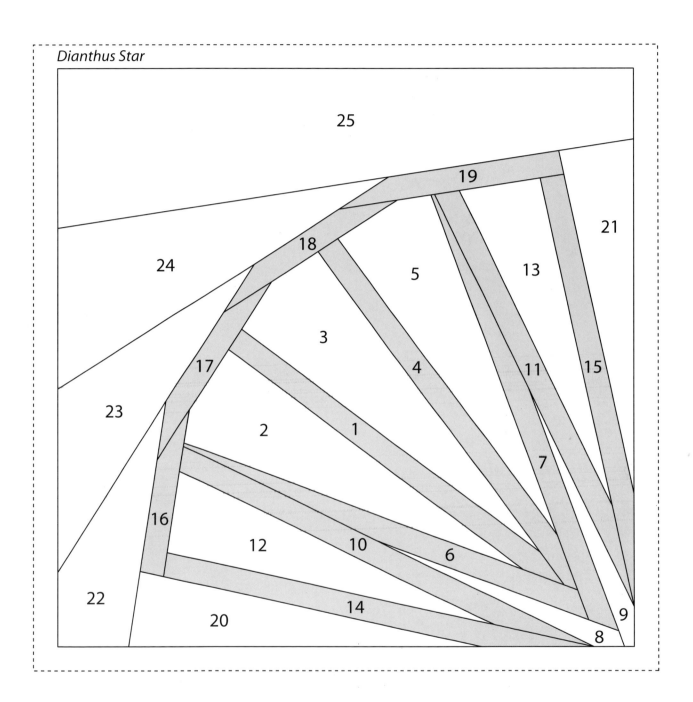

Dianthus Star

Freesia Star

Blooming in January and February indoors or in a greenhouse, freesias are irresistible. There is something extraordinarily spring-like in the sweet essence that pours from the flowers. Freesias come in a broad range of colors including: orange, pink, yellow, blue, purple, and white with tubular blossoms that line the long graceful stems. The bulbs are planted in pots in the late fall and early winter and treated in much the same way as tulips or hyacinths. Given lots of sun and cool temperatures, they will rapidly grow grass like leaves that give way to glorious flowers. For those of us who are impatient, a bunch of freesias from a florist will provide instant gratification.

Assembly

Make 4 of the foundation unit. Stitch the quarters together to make the block.

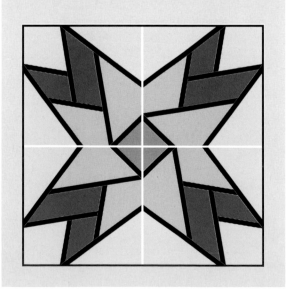

Yardage Requirements (for one block)

⅛ yd. black (leading)
⅛ yd. each pink, violet, and yellow
¼ yd. light blue floral (background)

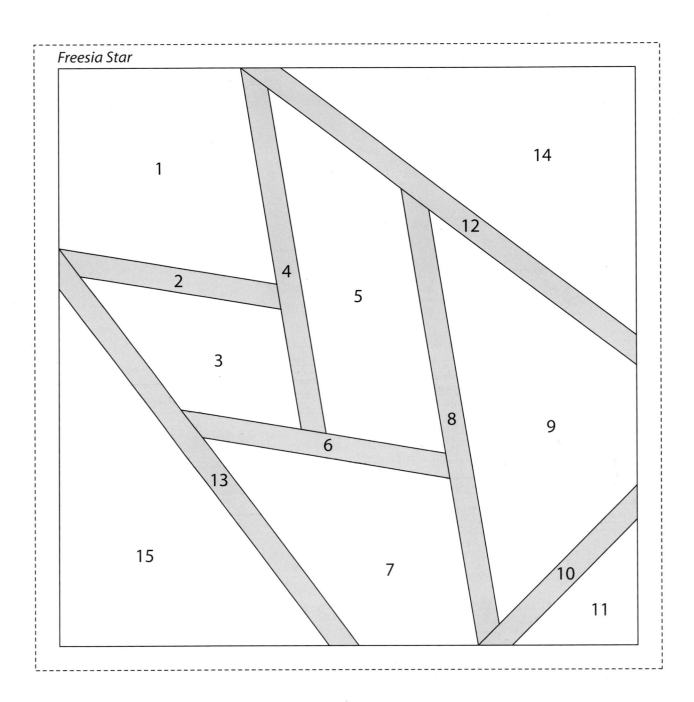

Freesia Star

1

14

12

2

4

5

3

8

9

6

13

15

7

10

11

Hibiscus Star

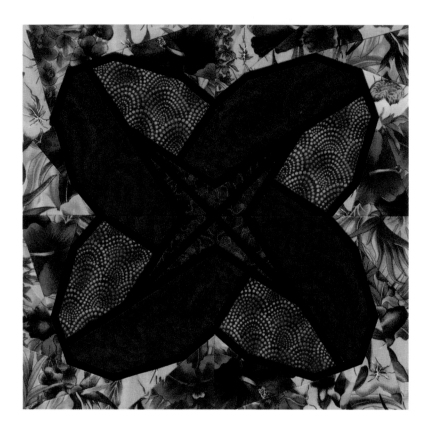

Hibiscus is a great plant for extravagant blooms and foliage. While the Chinese hibiscus is not winter hardy, it can be grown year-round in the greenhouse. It would be hard to imagine living in a tropical climate without these spectacular flowering plants. With flowers up to 8 inches across, they come in wonderful colors: electric pinks, intense reds, and startling yellow-orange combinations. The flowers usually last only for a day, but this is a small price to pay for a thing of such beauty. We like to keep some plants growing throughout the winter in the greenhouse where they thrive, but they will not put on their full show until summer when they are brought outside into full sun.

Assembly

Make 4 of the foundation unit. Stitch the quarters together to make the block.

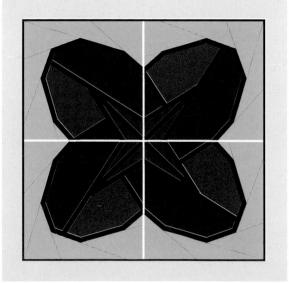

Yardage Requirements (for one block)

⅛ yd. black (leading)
⅛ yd. each red, yellow, and green
¼ yd. blue/red/yellow floral (background)

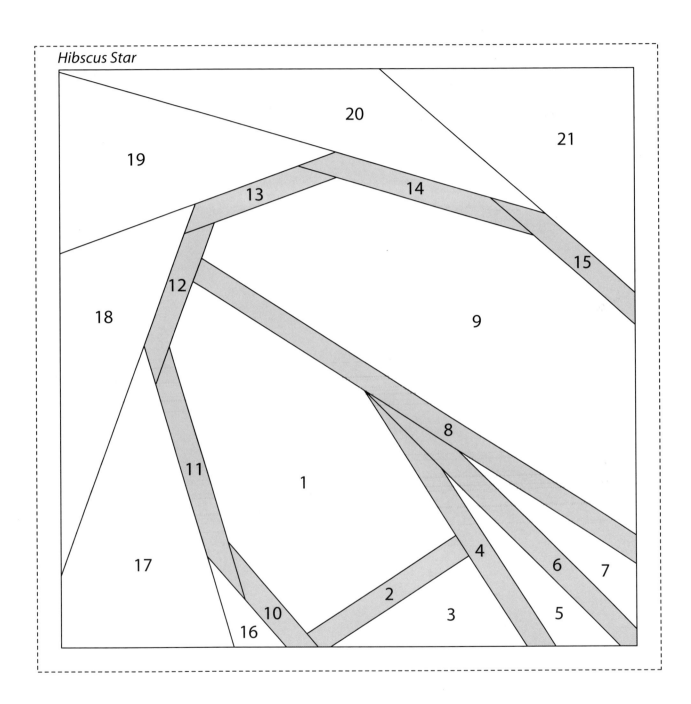

Hibscus Star

Hollyhock Star

Hollyhocks are available in a rich and varied range of colors including white, yellow, red, violet, purple, and almost black. They were especially popular garden flowers and reached their maximum popularity over a hundred years ago. In 1850, no English garden was without a collection of hollyhocks, but their use started to diminish at the beginning of this century. Possibly one reason for this is in their somewhat rustic aspect: in the 1800s people felt an affection for rustic effects in gardens. Today most of us consider hollyhocks as old-fashioned flowers, and when cultivated they are often grown in a spirit of nostalgia.

Assembly

Make 4 of the foundation unit. Stitch the quarters together to make the block.

Yardage Requirements (for one block)

⅛ yd. black (leading)
⅛ yd. each blue, purple and green floral
¼ yd. tan (background)

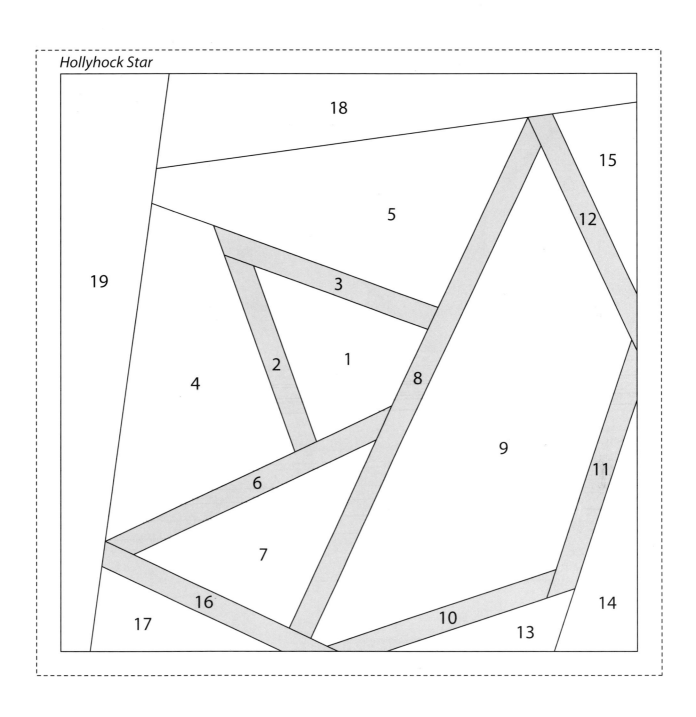

Hollyhock Star

Hydrangea Star

Hydrangeas are among the showiest of summer and autumn flowering woody plants. Shade tolerant, they grow well under trees or on the shady side of buildings. So popular at the turn of the century, gardeners are now planting them more than ever before. Hydrangeas have been the focus of modern plant breeders who have given us a huge selection of new colors and sizes to choose from. No longer available in just white and blue, all shades of pink, red, and lavender are now available. We like to grow the late flowering Pee Gee hydrangeas whose dried flower heads are ideal for arrangements.

Assembly

Make 4 of the foundation unit. Stitch the quarters together to make the block.

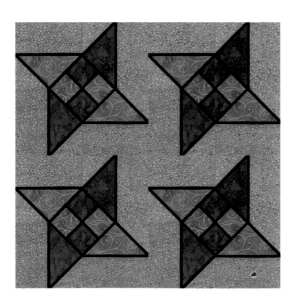

Yardage Requirements (for one block)

⅛ yd. black (leading)
⅛ yd. each medium blue and dark blue
¼ yd. beige floral (background)

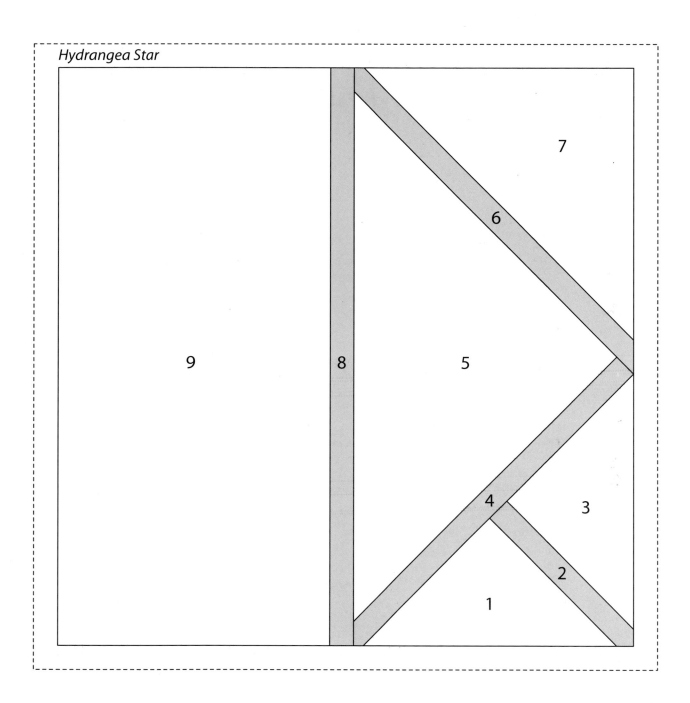

Hydrangea Star

Japanese Iris Star

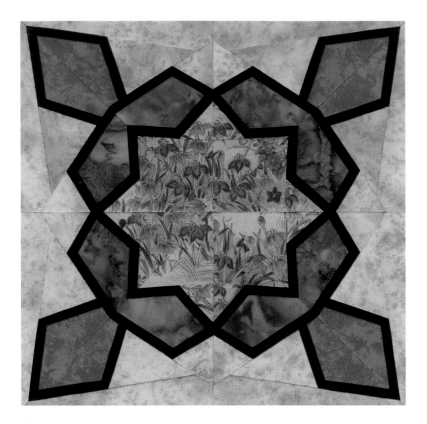

Blooming about a month later than the popular bearded iris, the Japanese irises are probably the most spectacular of all irises. The large flat flowers, up to 8 inches in diameter, are found in exquisite shades of blue, purple, pink, red, and white, either single or double, and often striped or marked in fantastic designs. The tall elegant foliage is also attractive. Some years ago we started some of these irises from seeds and planted them near our garden pond. They have since become the highlight of the June garden. Spending time in our gardens, whether it is fabric or soil, gives us an opportunity for self-renewal and peaceful contemplation. We hope our version will inspire you as well.

Assembly

Make 4 of foundation units A–D. Matching the lowercase letters in the seam allowances, join the units alphabetically. Stitch the quarters together.

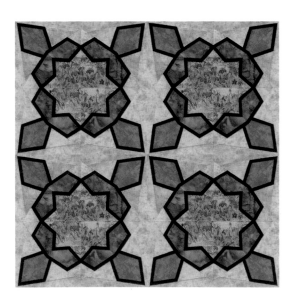

Yardage Requirements (for one block)

⅛ yd. black (leading)
⅛ yd. each light purple, medium purple, and tan floral print
¼ yd. mottled tan (background)

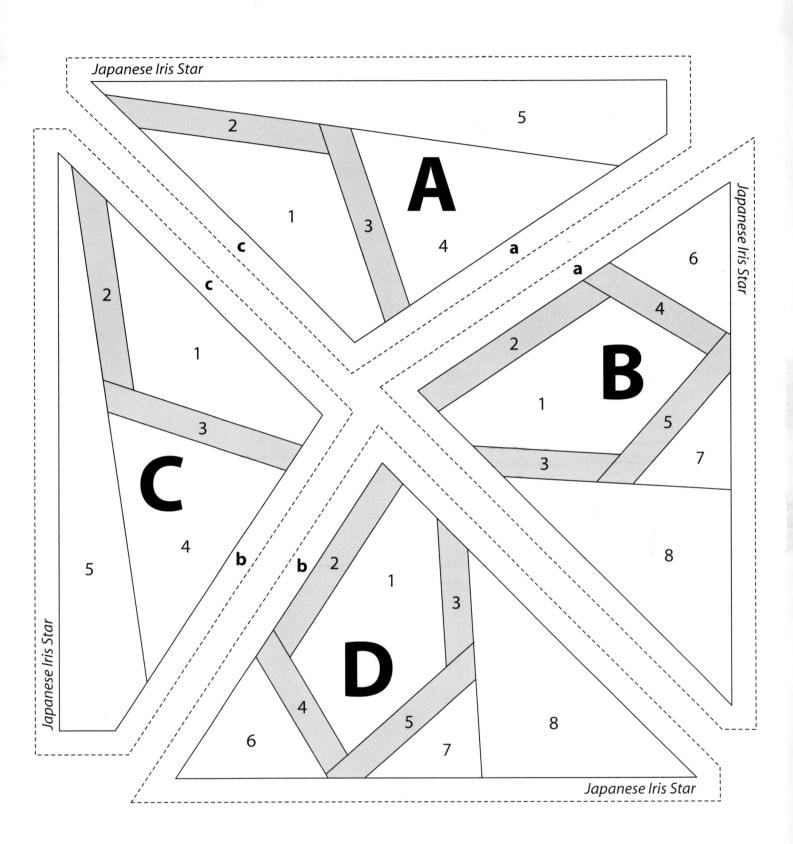

Japanese Iris Star

Japanese Iris Star

Japanese Iris Star

Japanese Iris Star

Lady's Slipper Star

Well known and beloved, the lady's slipper orchid inhabits arctic to subtropical North America, Europe, and Asia. Around 40 species can be found growing in forests, swamps, and bogs. Many of us, while walking through the woods, have been delighted by the appearance of a cluster of these striking orchids. As gardeners and flower lovers, our first impulse is to dig up a few to transplant in our garden. Sadly, they almost never survive the transplant and it only serves to endanger their numbers even more. As a child, I remember pink lady's slippers growing wild in the woods, blooming in the spring with a pinkish tan flower, and was the model for this star.

Assembly

Make 4 of foundation units A and B. Join the triangles to make a total of 4 squares. Sew the quarters together to make the block.

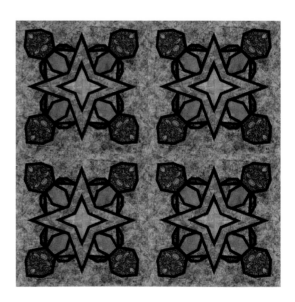

Yardage Requirements (for one block)

¼ yd. black (leading)
⅛ yd. each light purple, green, peach, and purple floral*
¼ yd. tan

*extra material may be needed to center floral motifs as shown in photos

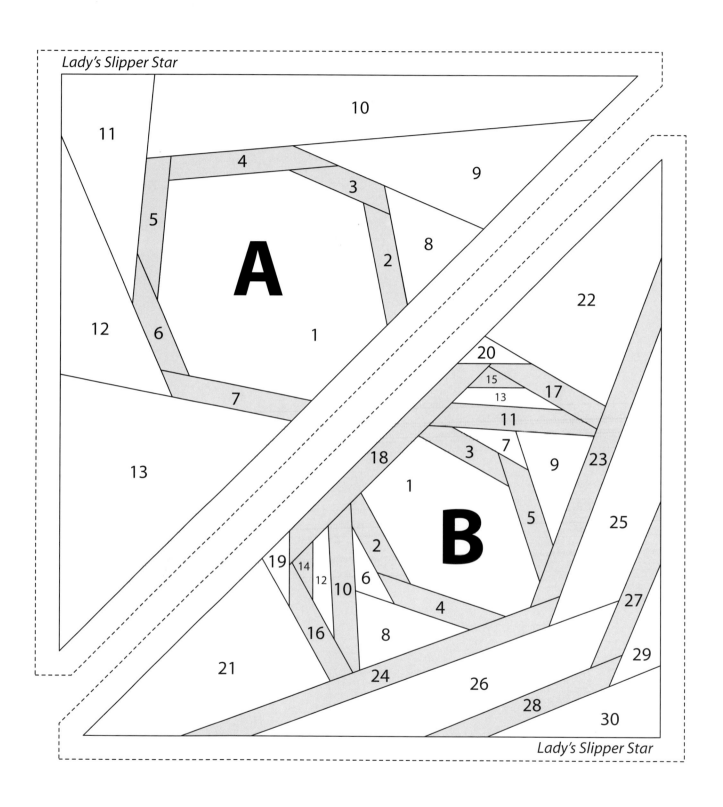

Lady's Slipper Star

Larkspur Star

Closely related to the perennial delphinium, the annual larkspur also prefers cool summers. Once planted, larkspurs will come back each year from self-sown seeds. Available in pinks, blues, and whites, we chose to show our larkspur in delicate pastels reminiscent of an English cottage garden. We like to grow them almost like a wildflower, letting them bloom without much attention. Even though their flowers cannot compete with the magnificent delphinium, larkspurs are lovely alternatives for lovers of a carefree annual cutting garden.

Assembly

Make 4 of the foundation unit. Stitch the quarters together to make the block.

Yardage Requirements (for one block)

¼ yd. black (leading)
⅛ yd. each peach, pink, and purple floral
¼ yd. dark tan (background)

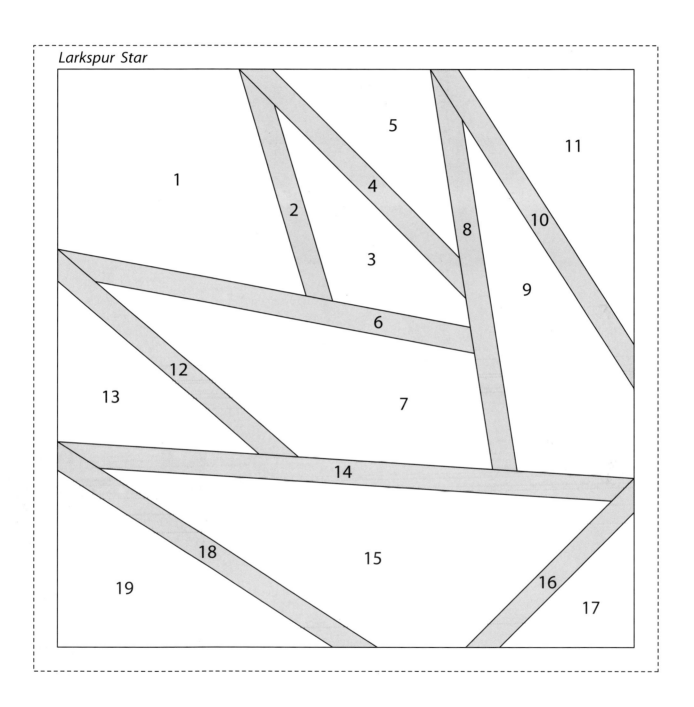

Larkspur Star

Lavender Star

Lavender, that lovely old-fashioned flower of cottage gardens has long been cultivated for its perfume. It is one of the oldest cultivated plants in the world. Even today, a luxurious haze of purple lavender is one of life's simple pleasures. There are many ways to enjoy the wonderful scent of lavender. Dried flower heads are a main ingredient of many potpourri recipes, and the oil has been used for centuries in soaps, creams, and perfumes. In the garden, lavender enjoys a sunny warm location and can live for many years. The best time to gather the flower spikes is before the florets are fully expanded, on cloudless mornings, and while they are still slightly damp from the dew.

Assembly

Make 4 of foundation units A and B. Join the triangles to make a total of 4 squares. Sew the quarters together to make the block.

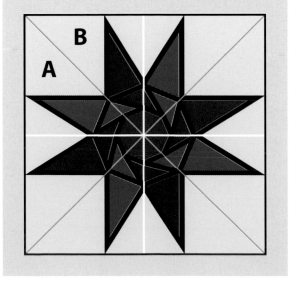

Yardage Requirements (for one block)

⅛ yd. black (leading)
⅛ yd. each medium purple, dark purple, and green floral
¼ yd. light purple (background)

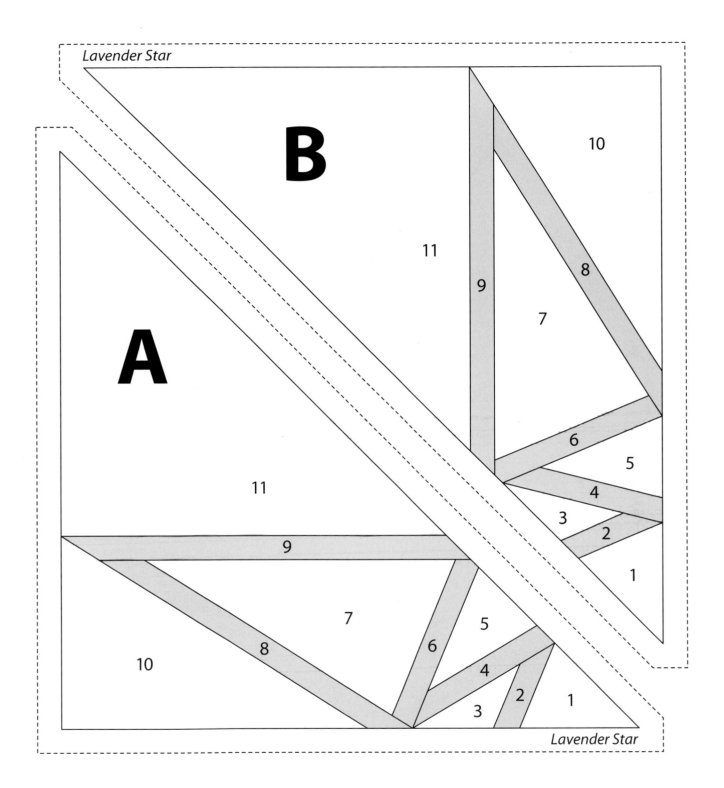

Lavender Star

B

A

Lavender Star

Lilac Star

Who can resist the smell of lilacs? It is a fragrance that is both relaxing and comforting. Early U.S. settlers brought lilacs from Europe, and even today while traveling through the countryside one can see them in full bloom beside the crumbling remains of foundations. Although their dominant shades of mauve, purple, and violet are the most common, they are available in white and pink as well. While lilacs are not difficult to grow, in order to bloom well they need full sun. At the turn of the century, lilacs were raised in greenhouses for winter cut flowers, a practice that is still popular in Europe.

Assembly

Make 4 of the foundation unit. Stitch the quarters together to make the block.

Yardage Requirements (for one block)

⅛ yd. black (leading)
⅛ yd. each light purple, gray, and pink
¼ yd. purple floral (background)

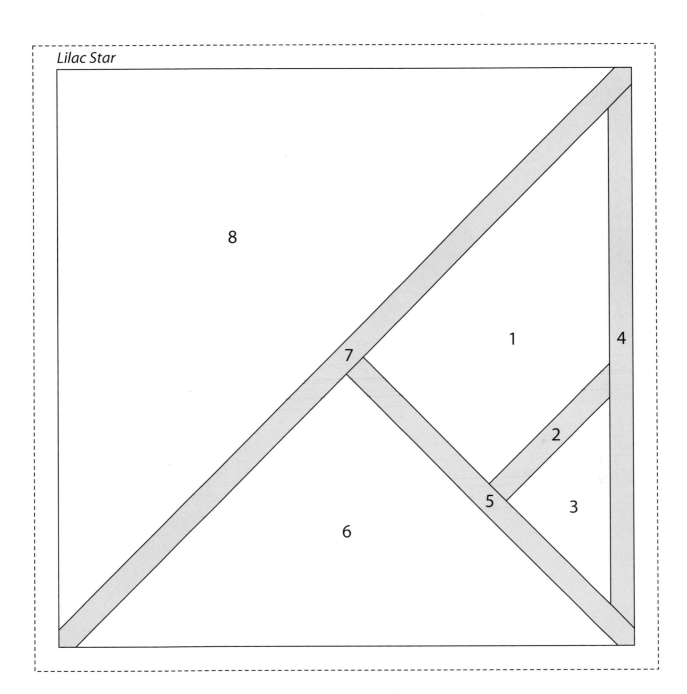

Lilac Star

Lily-of-the-Valley Star

Our late May garden heralds the return of the wonderfully perfumed lily-of-the-valley. A native of Britain, this tiny white, and less common pink, bell-shaped flower now grows almost everywhere in the temperate world. Already popular in the 1600s, the lily-of-the-valley was among the first flowers cultivated in English gardens. The little flowers were gathered and steeped in water for a month to make a solution called aqua aurea, and was used as a herbal remedy. Given a moist shady place, they will thrive and spread in the same spot, happily sharing space with larger shrubs and trees.

Assembly

Make 4 of foundation units A and B. Join the triangles to make a total of 4 squares. Sew the quarters together to make the block.

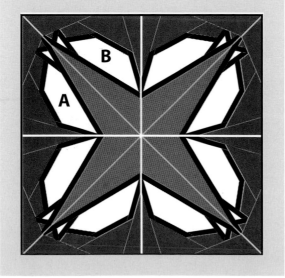

Yardage Requirements (for one block)

¼ yd. black (leading)
⅛ yd. green floral
¼ yd. each light brown (background) and white

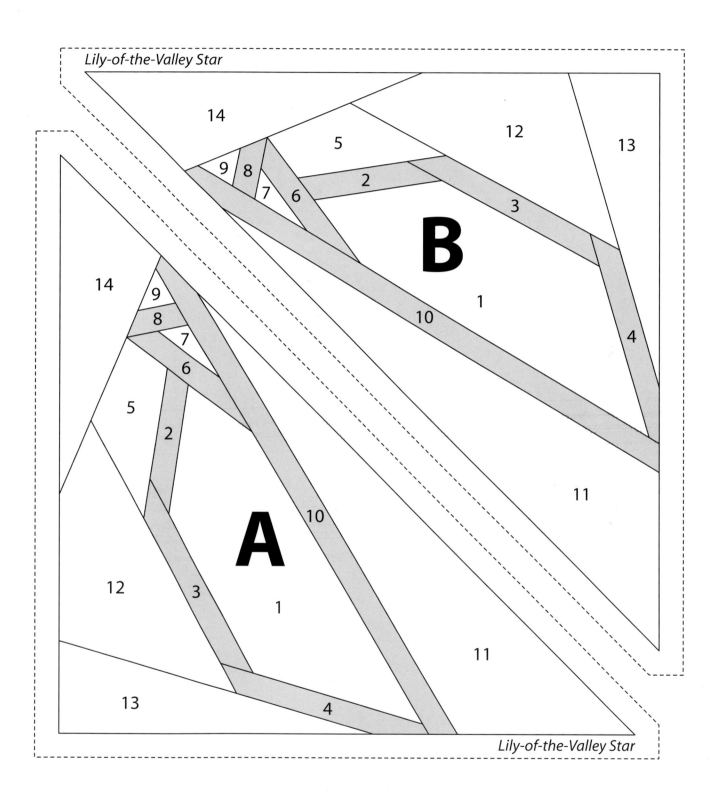

Lupine Star

Lupines are colorful aristocrats of the spring and summer garden. They bear dense spikes of pea-like flowers and do best in climates with warm sunny days and cool nights. The most popular garden varieties are the Russell hybrids. Easily raised from seeds, these rapidly growing plants produce spectacular 2-foot spires in shades of blue with white, carmine, red, yellow, and white. Some of our most beautiful wildflowers are members of the Lupine family. From the beloved Texas Blue Bonnets, to the wild blue lupines of Newfoundland, lupines are a source of sheer delight.

Assembly

Make 4 of foundation units A and B. Join the units to make a total of 4 squares. Sew the quarters together to make the block.

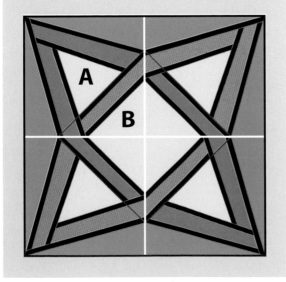

Yardage Requirements (for one block)

⅛ yd. black (leading)
⅛ yd. each lime green, blue, and beige floral*
¼ yd. gray (background)

*extra material may be needed to center floral motifs as shown in photos

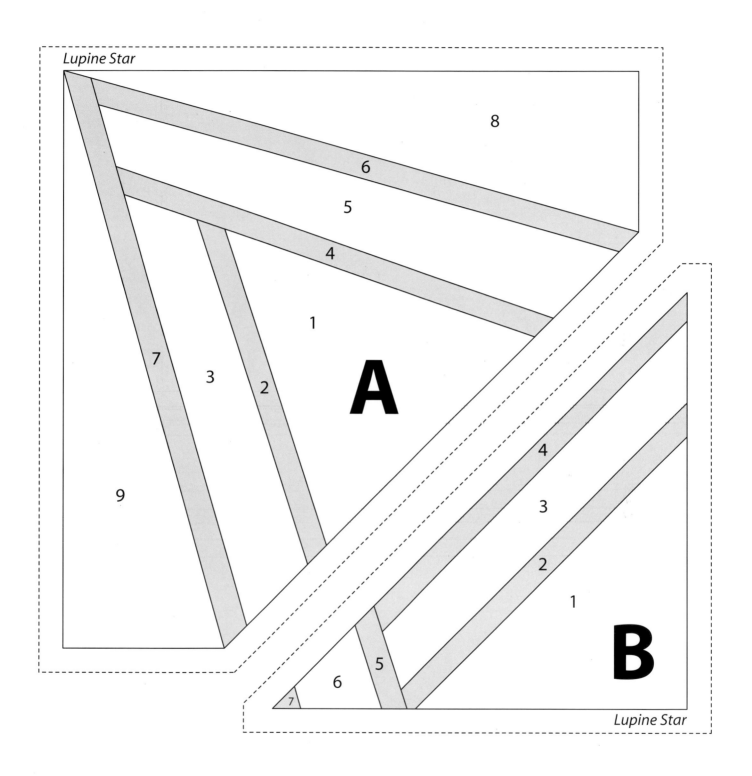

Lupine Star

8

6

5

4

1

7

3

2

A

9

4

3

2

1

5

6

7

B

Lupine Star

Magnolia Star

With their striking shapes, handsome bark, and foliage, magnolias are breathtaking in any garden or landscape. Interestingly, they are also among the most ancient of trees and shrubs, dating back to the earliest appearance of flowering plants in the fossil record. There are magnolias that are native to almost all parts of the world that enjoy a temperate climate. Varying in ultimate size from small shrubs to large trees, they are available in many colors including white, yellow, and many shades of rose and pink. In Virginia, we are able to grow the wonderfully scented Magnolia Grandiflora whose large white flowers and shiny evergreen leaves are treasures of the early summer garden.

Assembly

Make 4 of the foundation unit. Stitch the quarters together to make the block.

Yardage Requirements (for one block)

⅓ yd. black (leading)
⅛ yd. each green, yellow, purple, and peach
¼ yd. each white and tan floral (backround)

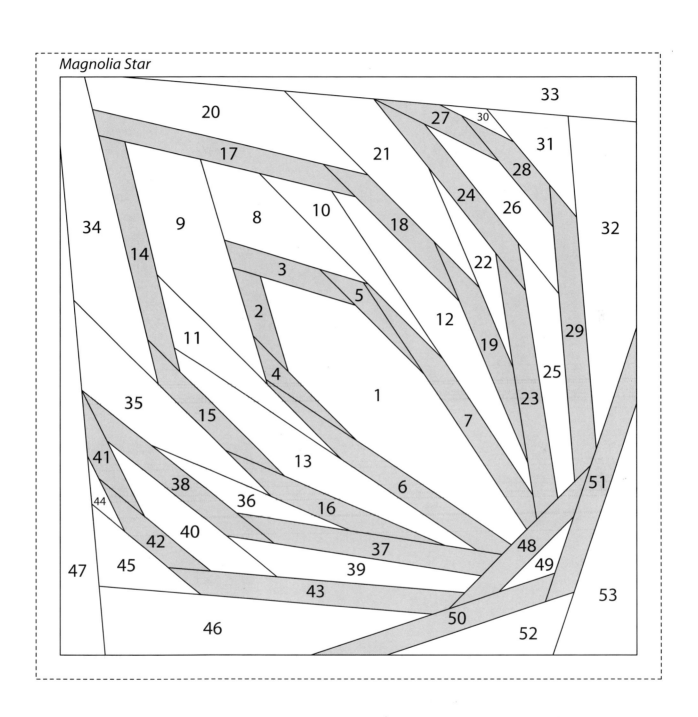

Magnolia Star

Mistletoe Star

Especially important at Christmas, mistletoe is known more for its white berries than its insignificant flower. The plant itself is actually a parasite, attaching itself to certain trees, such as oak and apple. The Druids held nothing more sacred than the mistletoe and according to legend they would use a golden sickle to cut it from the trees. In America, wherever mistletoe is hung, a kiss may be claimed from anyone standing under it. In many cultures mistletoe is used as a symbol of fertility. Even today in Australia, the aboriginal people believe that the spirits of children awaiting birth reside in mistletoe high up in the trees.

Assembly

Make 4 of foundation units A and B. Join the triangles to make a total of 4 squares. Sew the quarters together to make the block.

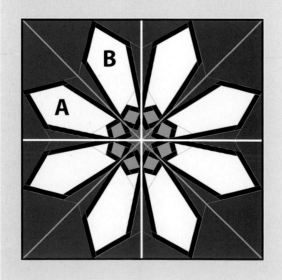

Yardage Requirements (for one block)

¼ yd. black (leading)
⅛ yd. each green and purple
¼ yd. each white and blue floral (background)

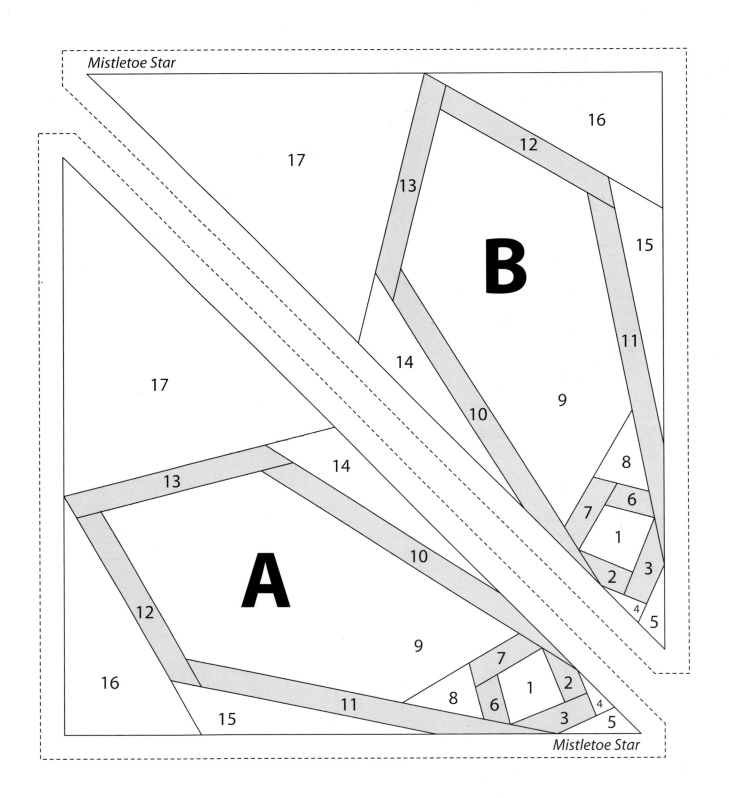

Mistletoe Star

Morning Glory Star

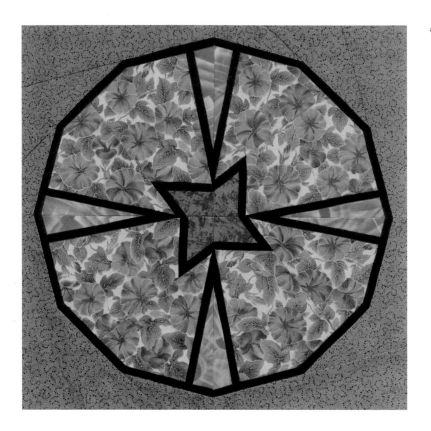

Native to the Americas, these trumpet flowers, on their climbing vines, open in the morning and close by midday. There is perhaps no more beautiful shade of blue than that of heavenly blue morning glories. Easily grown from large seeds, it is hard to imagine a summer without the sheer delight of entering the morning garden to be greeted by a bower of glorious sky blue morning glories. Several years ago, we grew a Japanese variety called Mt. Fuji, which produced magnificent blossoms in luminous shades of sky blue, violet, purple, pink and crimson, highlighted by a brilliant white pinwheel.

Assembly

Make 4 of the foundation unit. Stitch the quarters together to make the block.

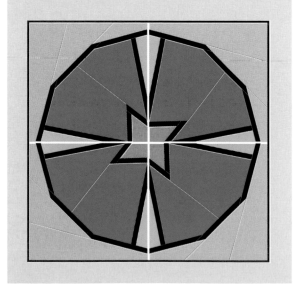

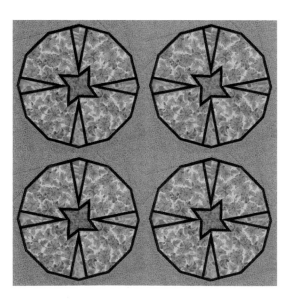

Yardage Requirements (for one block)

⅛ yd. black (leading)
⅛ yd. each light blue and yellow
¼ yd. each light green (background) and blue floral

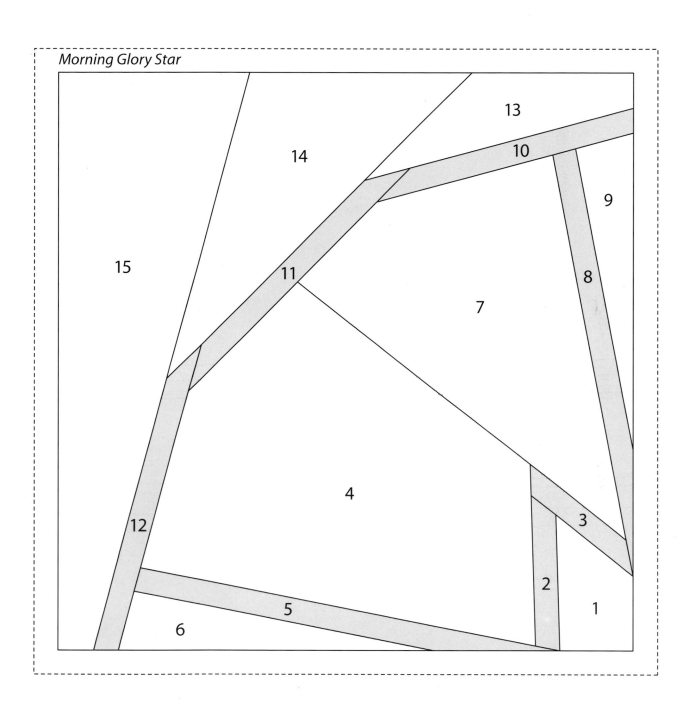

Morning Glory Star

Nasturtium Star

Nasturtiums, with their bright flowers and gracefully rounded leaves, tolerate poor soil, heat, and cold. They come in outstanding colors: deep rich yellows, oranges, and reds. They are great for beds and borders as well as hanging baskets and window boxes. In the kitchen, the edible leaves and flowers add a sweet and mildly spicy taste to salads and other dishes. The name nasturtium means "nose tormentor," a name given to the original wild flowers due to the biting peppery taste of their leaves. Native to Central America, they are usually grown from seeds directly planted into the ground.

Assembly

Make 4 of the foundation unit. Stitch the quarters together to make the block.

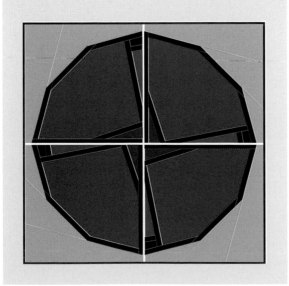

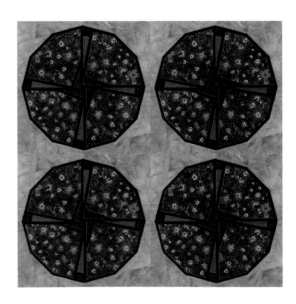

Yardage Requirements (for one block)

⅛ yd. black (leading)
⅛ yd. each green, orange and medium yellow
¼ yd. each light yellow (background) and orange floral print

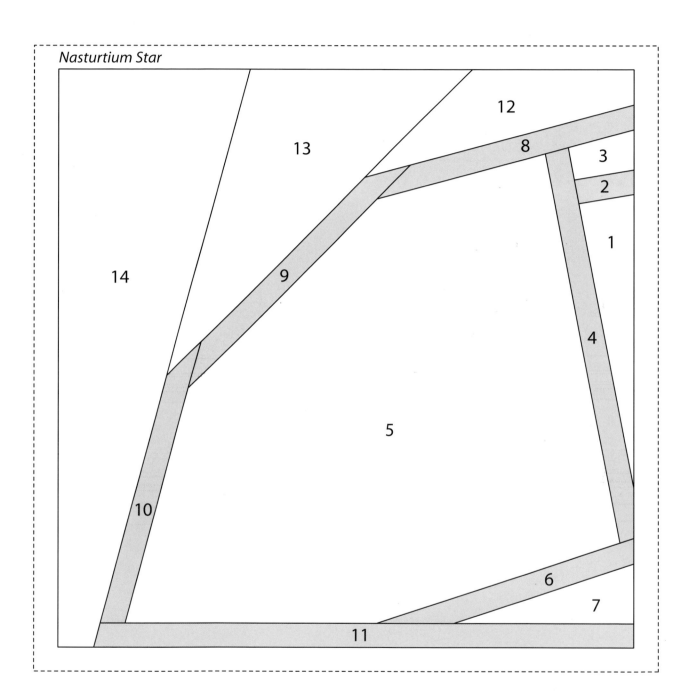

Nasturtium Star

Petunia Star

Today's petunias are descended from a weedy South American species collected about 200 years ago by French explorers. With familiar six packs available at almost every garden center in the spring, petunias are one of the most popular annuals. The color list continues to grow: all shades of pink and purple, white, yellow, but not a true blue. We like to plant them in containers, filled with rich soil, and place them in full sun. Nothing quite matches their exuberant blooms, which exude a lovely perfume on warm summer evenings.

Assembly

Make 4 of foundation units A and B. Join the triangles to make a total of 4 squares. Sew the quarters together to make the block.

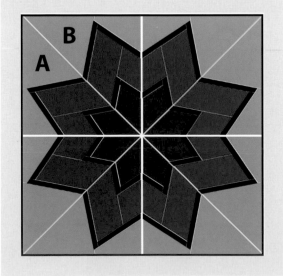

Yardage Requirements (for one block)

⅛ yd. black (leading)
⅛ yd. each dark blue and floral print
¼ yd. purple (background)

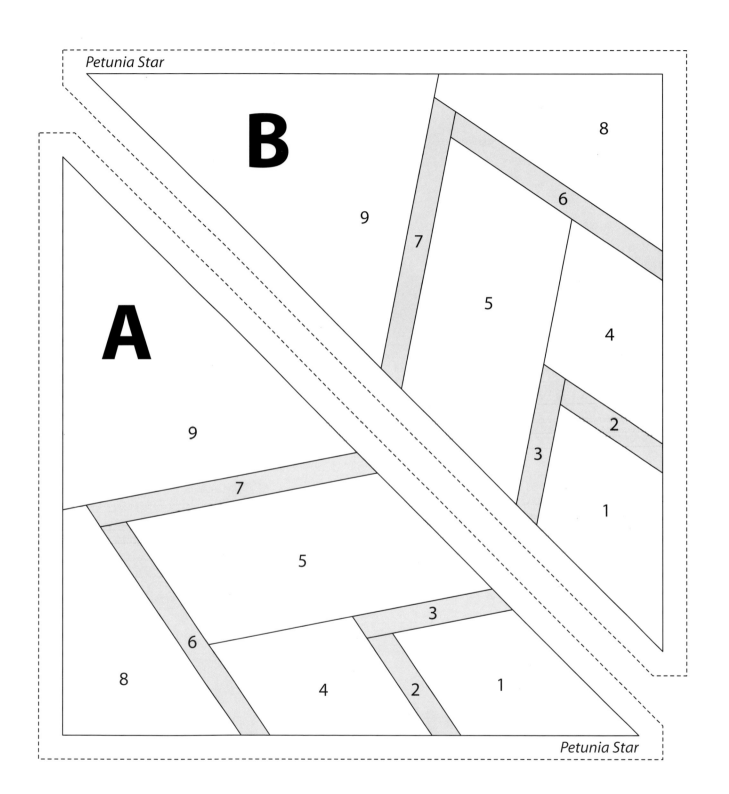

Petunia Star

B

8

9

6

7

5

4

2

3

1

A

9

7

5

6

3

8

4

2

1

Petunia Star

Plum Blossom Star

The plum blossom is one of the most frequently depicted of all subjects in Chinese floral art. Flowering in winter, the strongly scented flowers appear on apparently lifeless branches when snow and ice are still present, and no other plants are showing signs of spring. It shares the symbolism of the chrysanthemum which remains in bloom after other flowers have finished. It is seen to embody the virtues of purity and the ability to endure hardship. Traditionally shown as white, our interpretation of this lovely flower is done in soft shades of purple, blue, green, and mauve. For us, it is conducive to restoring inner calm and uplifting our spirits as winter draws to a close.

Assembly

Make 4 of the foundation unit. Stitch the quarters together to make the block.

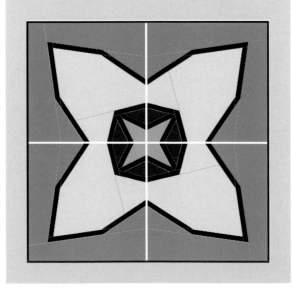

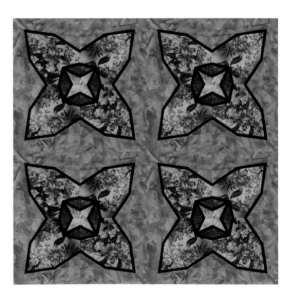

Yardage Requirements (for one block)

⅛ yd. black (leading)
⅛ yd. each pink and purple
¼ yd. each violet (background) and tan floral

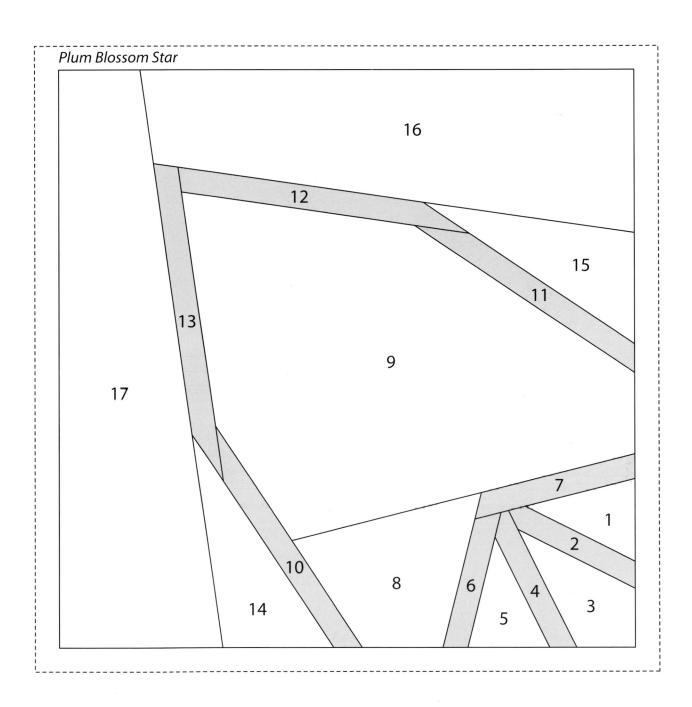

Plum Blossom Star

Poinsettia Star

It would be hard to imagine Christmas without poinsettias. A winter-flowering shrub, it originally came from Mexico and was introduced to the trade about 1830. Not just red anymore, poinsettias now come in various shades of white and pink. The true flowers are the tiny yellow balls that are clustered in the center of the bracts, which are actually brightly colored leaves. Long thought to be poisonous, recent evidence has shown this to be false. Many people coax their plants to continue growing throughout the year and even have them bloom again.

Assembly

Make 4 of foundation units A and B. Join the triangles to make a total of 4 squares. Sew the quarters together to make the block.

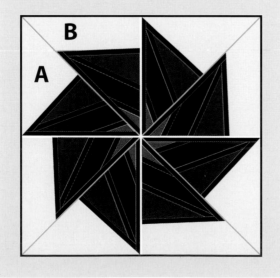

Yardage Requirements (for one block)

¼ yd. black (leading)
⅛ yd. each red, green, and yellow
¼ yd. cream floral (background)

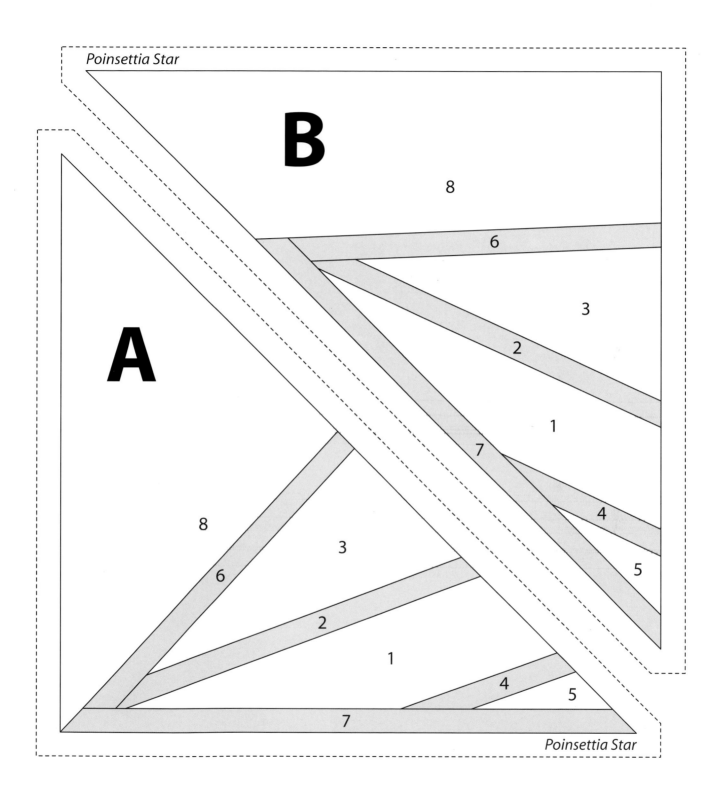

Poinsettia Star

B

8

6

3

2

1

7

4

5

A

8

3

6

2

1

7

4

5

Poinsettia Star

Poppy Star

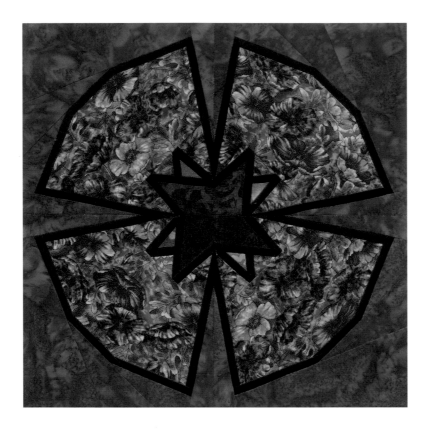

Cultivation of poppies dates back to the remotest antiquity. The flowers, its seeds, and the sap of certain species provided most of the ancient world with an important religious symbol, a palatable foodstuff, and a narcotic. Today in some parts of the world opium poppies are still grown, but we who are gardeners appreciate poppies for their floral beauty. We grow two types of poppies; the Oriental poppy, a perennial whose bright orange and red flowers last but a week at the end of May and annual Iceland poppies which are available in a spectrum of blazing colors. In some states, they can be found along roadsides and medians where they delight the passing motorist.

Assembly

Make 4 of the foundation unit. Stitch the quarters together to make the block.

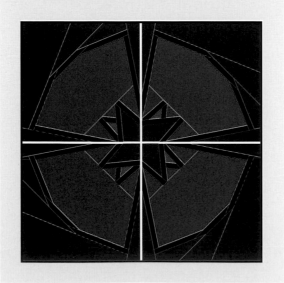

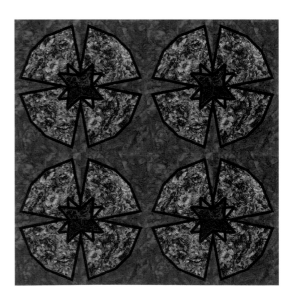

Yardage Requirements (for one block)

⅛ yd. black (leading)
⅛ yd. each orange and yellow
¼ yd. each purple (background) and orange floral print

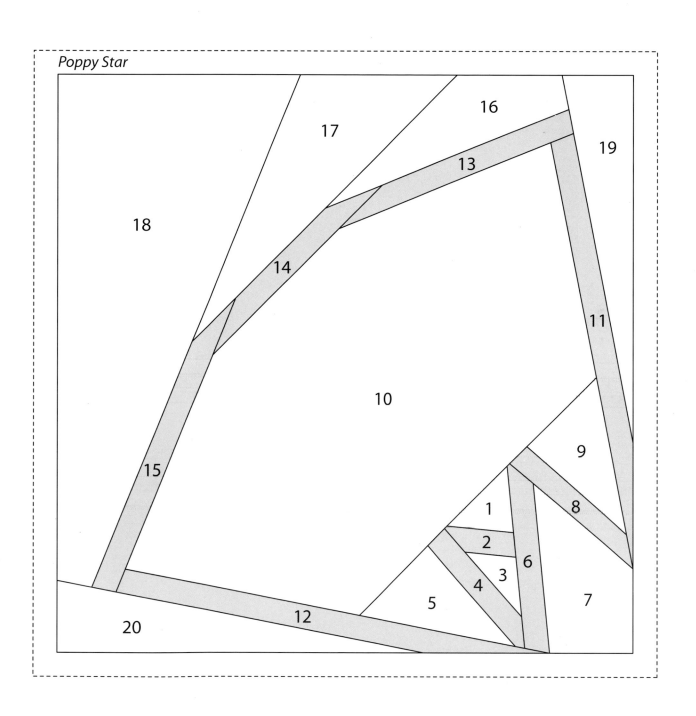

Poppy Star

Prickly Pear Star

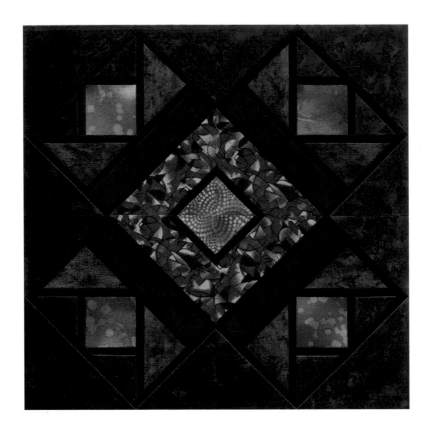

The prickly pear cactus has round, flattened pads, and often bears spiny edible fruits. Driving around the Southeast in the late spring, we noticed mounded cactus like plants covered with bright yellow flowers and later found out that these were prickly pear cacti. We were surprised that these plants would survive in this part of the country, which is neither excessively hot nor dry. Many people have a love-hate relationship with cacti. While some have yards and greenhouses full, others would not allow a plant near them. We enjoy the wonderful bright yellow flowers, but make no mistake—they must be handled with extreme care!

Assembly

Make 4 of the foundation unit. Stitch the quarters together to make the block.

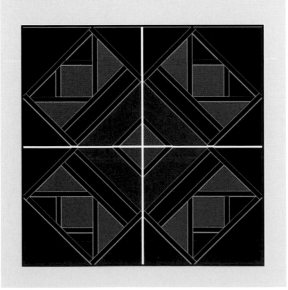

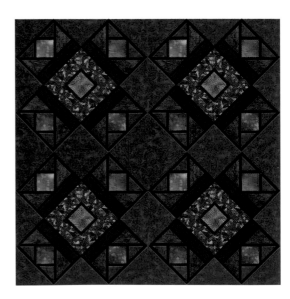

Yardage Requirements (for one block)

⅛ yd. black (leading)
⅛ yd. each red, orange, yellow, light green, and multi-color floral
¼ yd. dark blue (background)

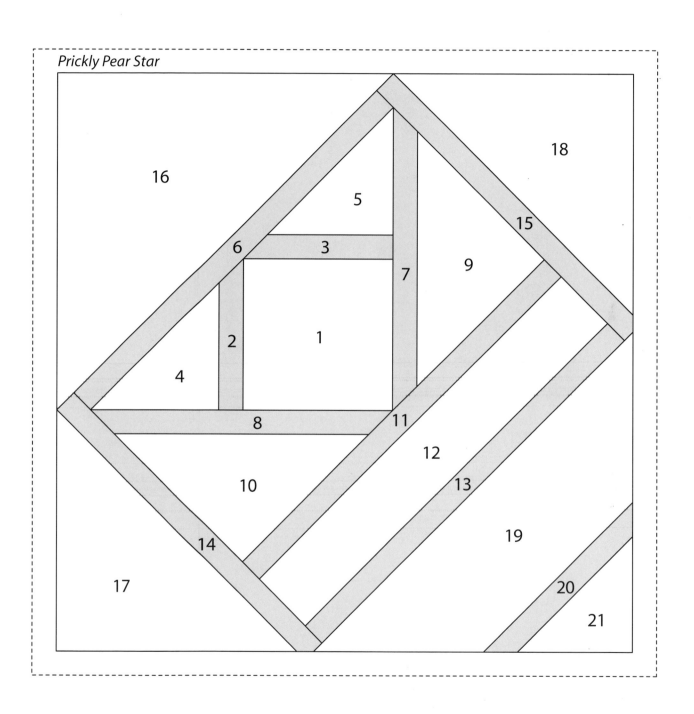

Prickly Pear Star

Primrose Star

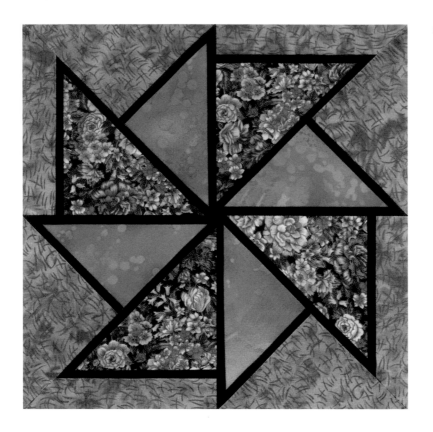

Primroses are beloved spring flowers that bloom with flowering bulbs when the earth is reawakening. The broad leaves rise directly from the stout crowns with fibrous roots. The flowers are tubular with five flattened petals, found in open branched clusters or whirled tiers. Most are native to cool regions and dislike high heat and humidity. In Western and Southern Europe, the common, or English primrose is one of the best known of all wildflowers in the world. It is held in affection by flower lovers for its welcome carpet of yellow blooms in February or March. In the United States, we are more apt to see primroses sold in pots, like miniature bouquets in a wide array of jewel tone colors.

Assembly

Make 4 of foundation units A and B. Join the triangles to make a total of 4 squares. Sew the quarters together to make the block.

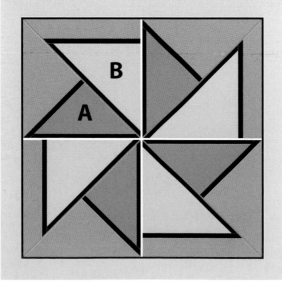

Yardage Requirements (for one block)

⅛ yd. black (leading)
⅛ yd. each light pink and dark pink floral
¼ yd. tan (background)

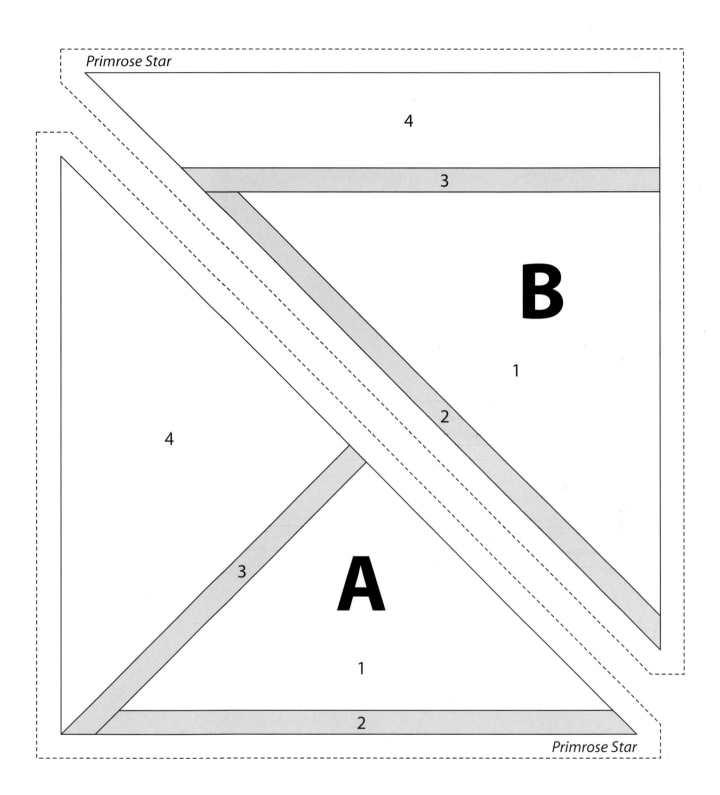

Primrose Star

4

3

B

1

2

4

3

A

1

2

Primrose Star

Queen Anne's Lace Star

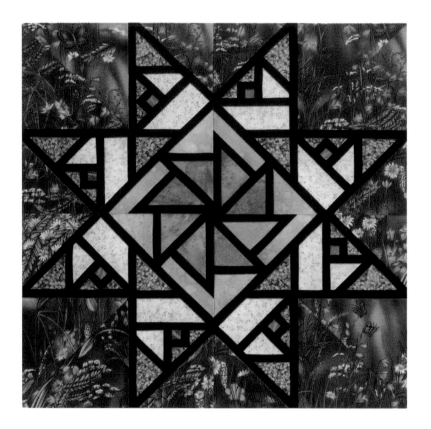

Have you ever driven down a country road in mid summer only to be captivated by billowing waves of Queen Anne's lace? It is hard to imagine that these breathtaking flowers are considered weeds. Technically, wildflowers are plants native to the area. Naturalized plants, also known to some of us as weeds, are the proper name for such roadside aliens like Queen Anne's lace. If such invaders can share the same spot with their native friends without taking over, all is well in the meadow. I find it hard to call this beauty an undesirable. The flower shape of this plant is an umbel, and inspired us to create the lovely pattern in our version of this elegant flower.

Assembly

Make 4 of units A–C. Matching the lower-case letters in the seam allowance of the sections, join them in alphabetical order. Stitch the block quarters together.

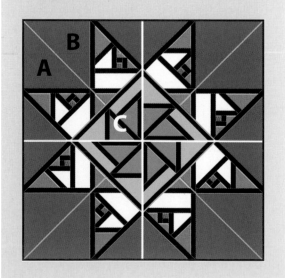

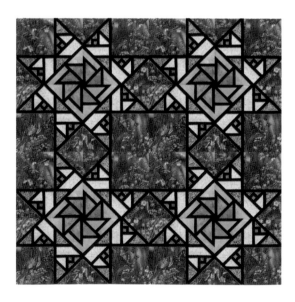

Yardage Requirements (for one block)

⅓ yd. black (leading)
⅛ yd. each light green, tan, pink, blue and white
¼ yd. green floral (background)

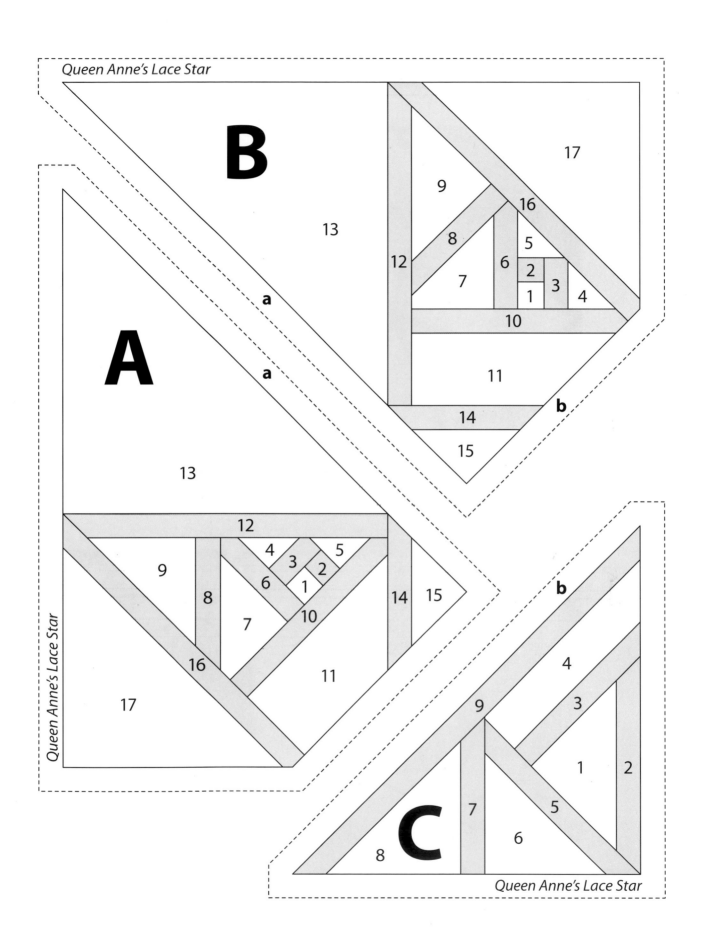

Queen Anne's Lace Star

B

17

9

16

13

12

8

5

6

2

7

1

3

4

10

11

14

b

15

A

a

a

13

12

4

5

9

3

2

8

6

1

7

10

14

15

16

11

17

Queen Anne's Lace Star

b

9

4

3

7

1

2

6

5

8

C

Queen Anne's Lace Star

Rhododendron Star

Growing rhododendrons can be contagious. Hybridizers have shown more interest in this genus, then perhaps all other shrubs. Evidence of hybrid plants among the Krume azaleas in Japanese gardens dates back to the seventeenth century. The nineteenth century began a busy time for breeders in England and Europe as explorers brought back an increasing number of new plant species. Today, rhododendrons are available in a tremendous diversity of flower colors and sizes, plant sizes, foliage, cold hardiness, heat tolerance, and disease resistance. The native light pink rhododendrons of our own Blue Ridge mountains were the inspiration for this block.

Assembly

Make 4 each of foundation units A and B. Stitch the sections together to make a total of 4 units. Join the quarters to make the block.

Yardage Requirements (for one block)

⅛ yd. black (leading)
⅛ yd. each pink and light pink floral
¼ yd. green (background)

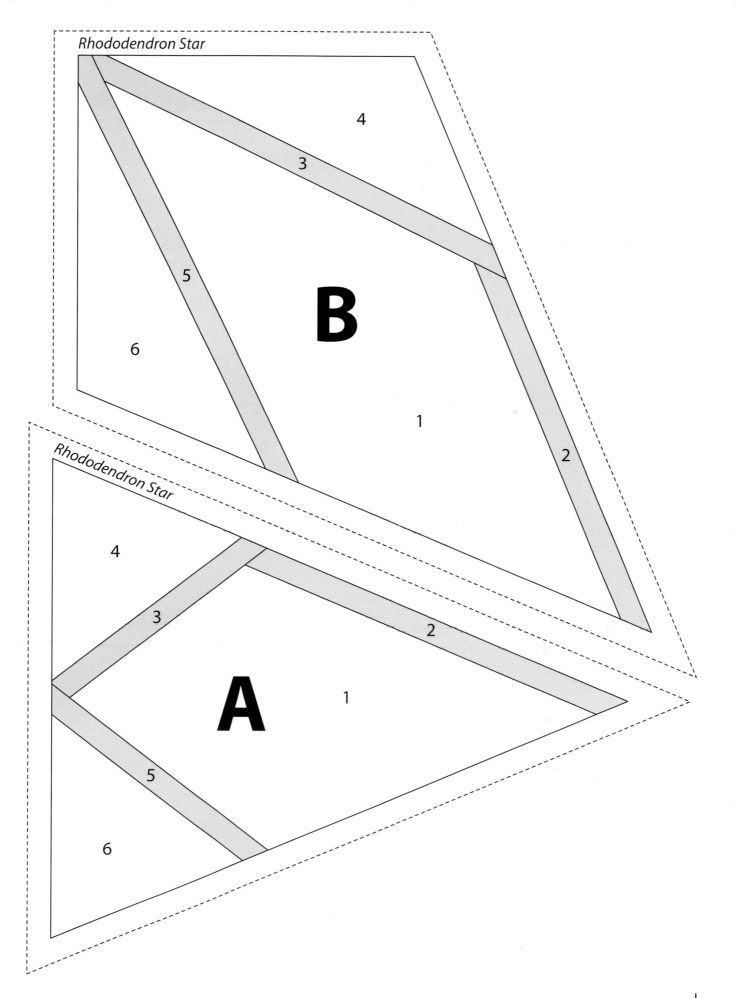

Rhododendron Star

B

4

3

5

6

1

2

Rhododendron Star

A

4

3

5

6

1

2

Saguaro Star

The celebrated saguaro cactus of the Arizona desert is an erect dark green tree-like giant that can grow over 50 feet tall and weigh many thousands of pounds. In its natural habitat, it is home to many birds and provides food for a great number of species. The white flowers are about 4 inches across and open at night. It is one of the giants in the cactus family, but is neither the tallest, nor heaviest. However, it is one of the most promoted, more often used as scenery in movies than any other cactus species. It can easily be propagated from seeds, but can take hundreds of years to reach maturity.

Assembly

Make 4 of units A and B. Stitch the units together to make a total of 4 quarters. Join the quarters to make the block.

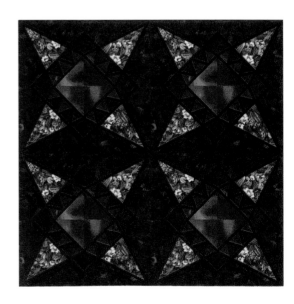

Yardage Requirements (for one block)

⅛ yd. black (leading)
⅛ yd. each orange, yellow, green, and light green floral
¼ yd. brown

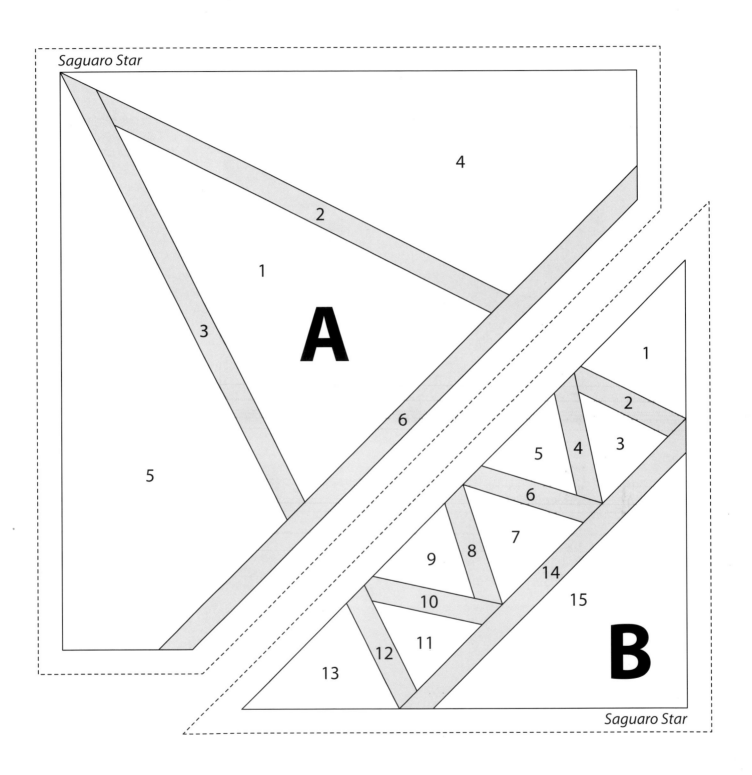

Saguaro Star

Saguaro Star

Strawflower Star

Native to Australia and thriving in sultry conditions, strawflowers or everlastings are the perfect choice for areas with long hot summers. These branched plants grow 12 to 30 inches tall and have narrow leaves with wiry stems bearing flowers of red, salmon, purple, yellow, pink, or white from July to frost. The colored parts of the flower are actually bracts with the true flowers in the center, much like the poinsettia. I plant them in rows in the vegetable patch, just to pick and dry for permanent bouquets. Why not create your own everlasting bouquet with fabric and thread by stitching this lovely block.

Assembly

Make 4 of foundation units A and B. Join the triangles to make a total of 4 squares. Sew the quarters together to make the block.

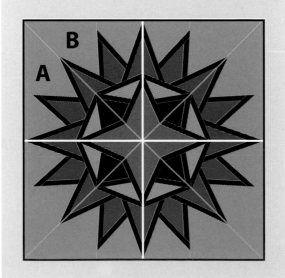

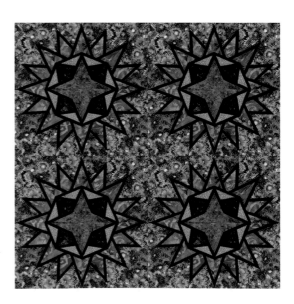

Yardage Requirements (for one block)

¼ yd. black (leading)
⅛ yd. each red, pink, peach, and purple
¼ yd. pink floral print (background)

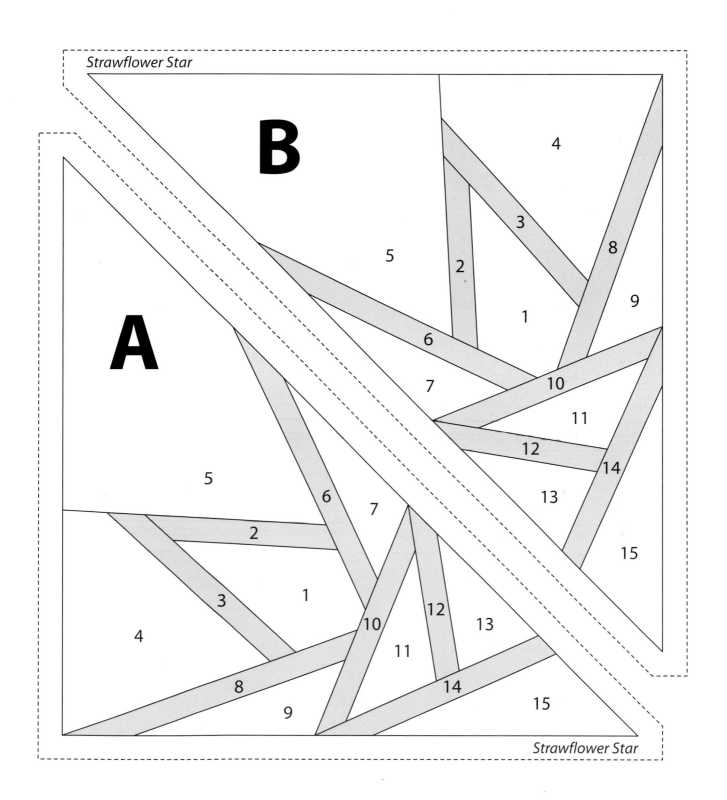

Strawflower Star

B

4

3

8

5

2

9

1

6

7

10

11

12

14

13

15

A

5

6

7

2

1

3

10

12

13

4

11

8

14

9

15

Strawflower Star

Sunflower Star

Sunflowers have never been so popular as they are today. Everyone from young children to adults adore them. Pick up your latest seed catalog and you will be amazed at the number of colors and sizes available: from white to every possible shade of yellow and gold to rich burgundies and reds. We look forward to the incredible bouquets we make in the summer by mixing all of those luscious colors together. Whether you prefer the 2-foot dwarfs, or the 10-foot giants, sunflowers are sure to give you a sunny disposition.

Assembly

Make 4 of foundation units A and B. Join the triangles to make a total of 4 squares. Sew the quarters together to make the block.

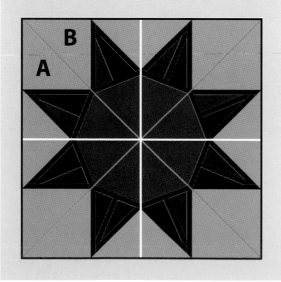

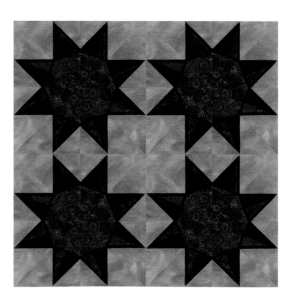

Yardage Requirements (for one block)

⅛ yd. black (leading)
⅛ yd. each burgundy, dark yellow and rust floral
¼ yd. green (background)

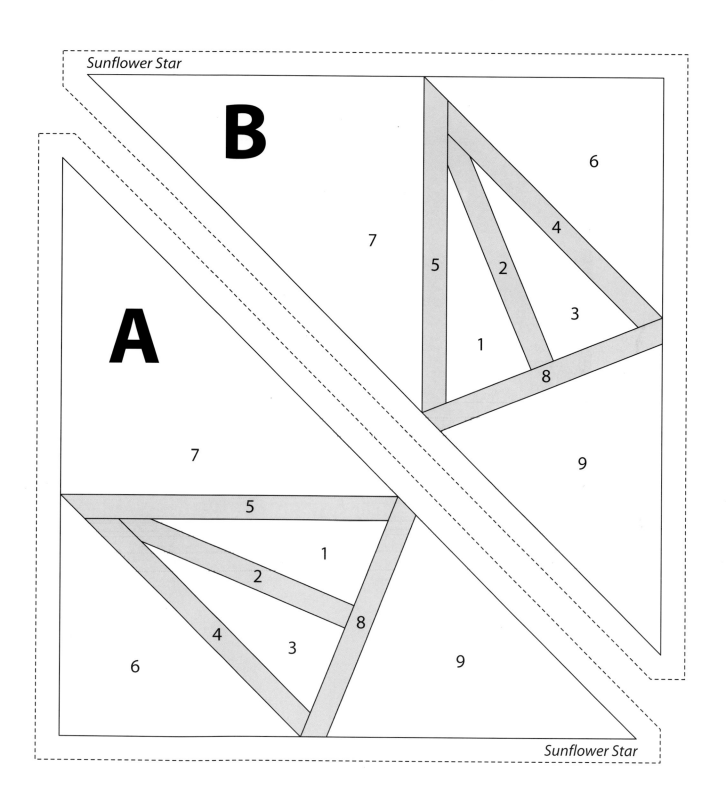

Sunflower Star

B

A

Sunflower Star

Toad Lily Star

In the fall, as our woodland garden begins to go to sleep for the winter, there appears curious maroon spotted flowers known as Tricyrtis. Also called toad lilies, perhaps because their speckled flowers resemble a toad's skin, they are best planted where they can be appreciated at close range: where one can get close to the flowers which are more unusual than showy. They also come in purple, lilac, and shades of pink as well as maroon. Widely available through mail order catalogs, these plants enjoy an evenly moist humus rich soil in a spot with dappled shade. In our garden, they share space with ferns and hardy cyclamen.

Assembly

Make 4 of foundation units A and B. Join the triangles to make a total of 4 squares. Sew the quarters together to make the block.

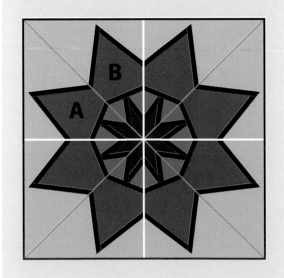

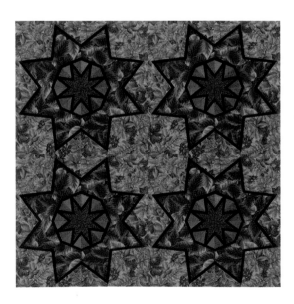

Yardage Requirements (for one block)

⅛ yd. black (leading)
⅛ yd. each brown, burgundy, and green
¼ yd. tan floral (background)

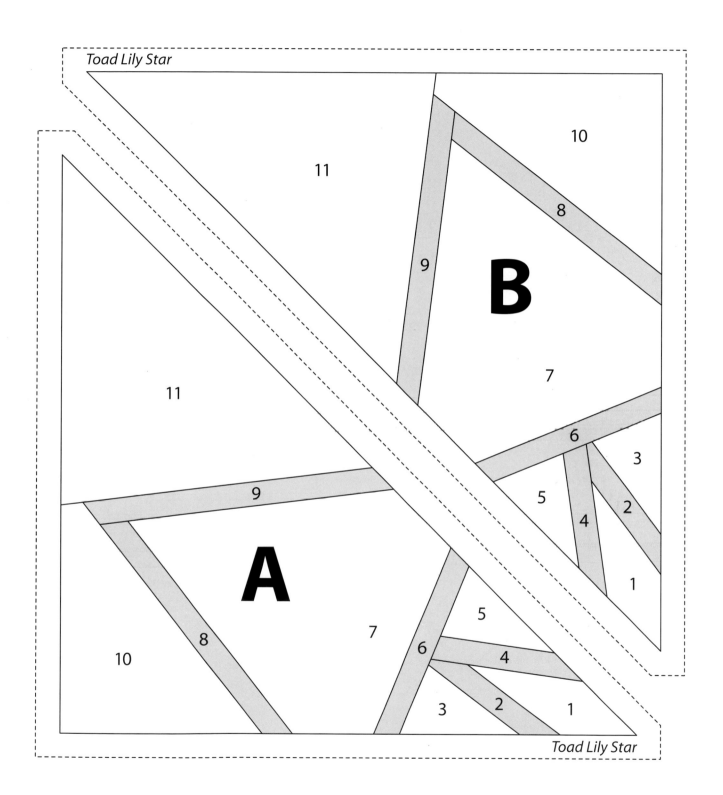

Toad Lily Star

Tulip Star

Whenever I see tulips, I think of tulipomania—the period in 17th century Holland, where at one point a house was traded for a rare tulip bulb. Dutch gardeners, not aware that a virus spread by aphids caused the colorful mutations, eagerly anticipated the chance that one of their bulbs might "break" into a form that could be propagated and sold for an outrageous fortune. The Dutch were entranced by the streaked and feathered variety known today as Rembrandt tulips because they were so often portrayed in paintings of the period. With their disarmingly simple shape, kaleidoscope of colors, and early blooming season, they are adored by gardeners everywhere.

Assembly

Make 4 of the foundation unit. Stitch the quarters together to make the block.

Yardage Requirements (for one block)

¼ yd. black (leading)
⅛ yd. each blue, green, and yellow
¼ yd. light blue (background) and yellow floral

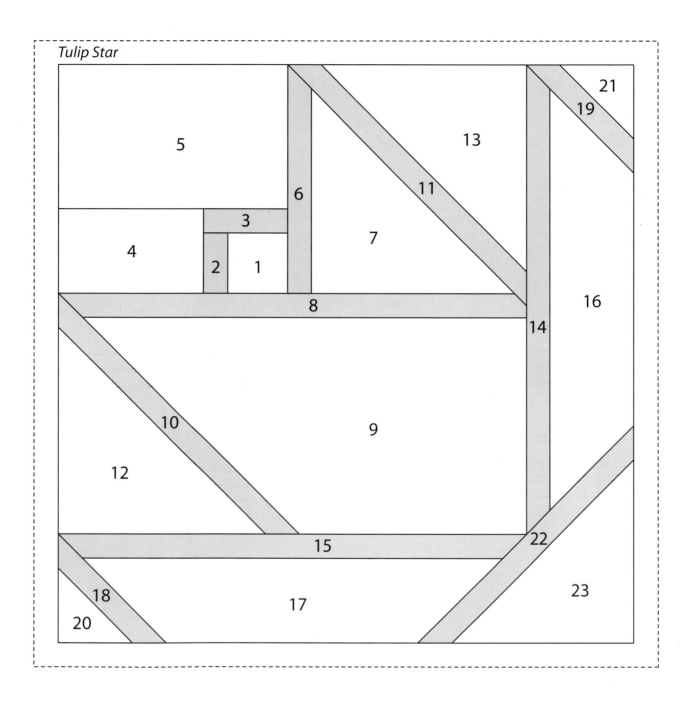

Tulip Star

Viola Star

The genus Viola is very large and includes both pansies and violets. Over five hundred species of this old-fashioned plant have been documented. Much like the daisy, people tend to embrace some species while considering others obnoxious weeds. The familiar Johnny jump ups, with their happy faces of purple and yellow, are the inspiration for our block. Reminding me of Easter, I love the rich combination of purples, blues, and yellows. Like many of the other flowers in this book, violas prefer cool climates. In the *Oddessy*, Homer states that the sweet smelling violet, Viola odorata, was among the flowers and plants on the fair island of the seductive nymph, Calypso.

Assembly

Make 4 of foundation units A and B. Join the triangles to make a total of 4 squares. Sew the quarters together to make the block.

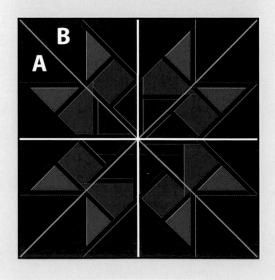

Yardage Requirements (for one block)

⅛ yd. black (leading)
⅛ yd. each burgundy, yellow, green, and purple
¼ yd. floral print (background)

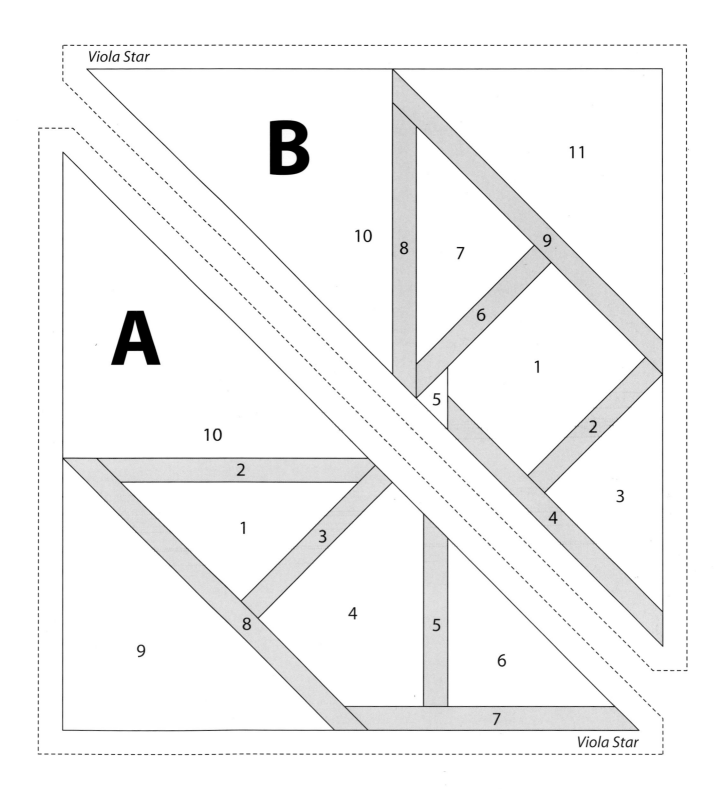

Viola Star

B

A

11

10

8   7   9

6

1

5

2

10   3

2

1   4

3

4

8

5

9   6

7

Viola Star

Wild Rose Star

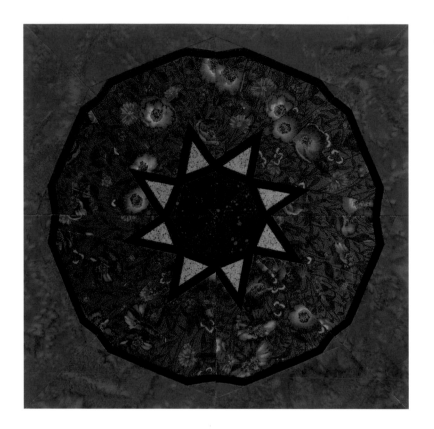

In the 1920s, Gertrude Stein wrote, "Rose is a rose is a rose is a rose," and probably she had nothing else in mind but this flower. It is indeed the only thing to be said about a rose, other than writing a whole poem about it. The essence of a rose is unattainable, mysterious, and even more of a mystery is that it can never be accurately described by words alone. Roses are romantic, steeped in sentiment—true flowers of the Victorian era. Still popular today, roses are loved by many people, and are perhaps the most beloved of any flower. The pink and red single flowering shrub roses were the inspiration for this lovely design.

Assembly

Make 4 each of the foundation units A and B. Stitch the sections together to make a total of 4 units. Join the quarters to make the block.

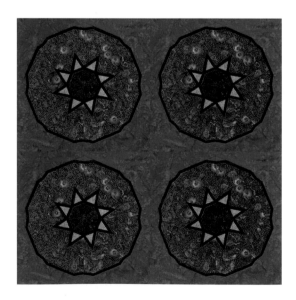

Yardage Requirements (for one block)

⅛ yd. black (leading)
⅛ yd. each red, yellow, and green floral
¼ yd. blue (background)

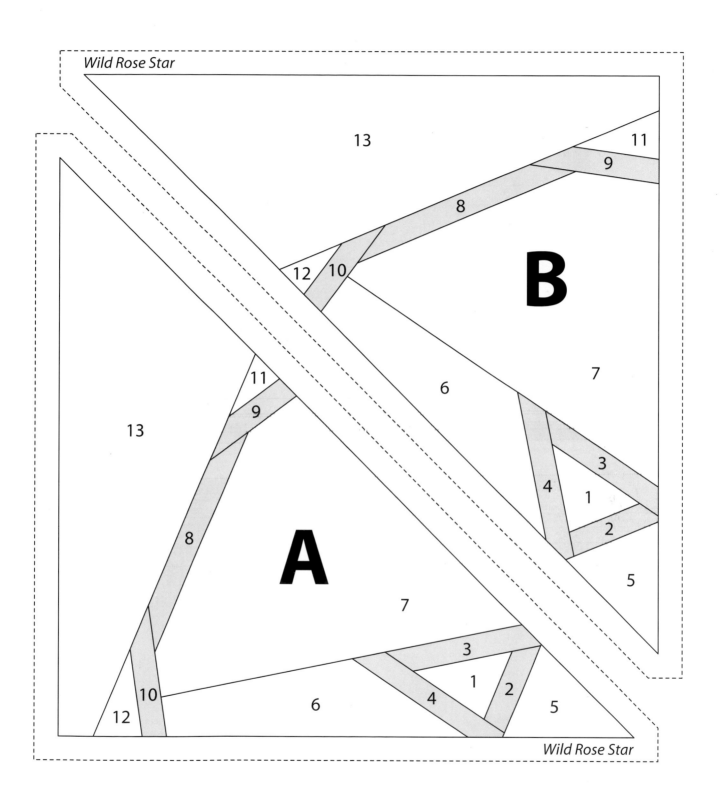

Wild Rose Star

13

11

9

8

12 10

B

7

6

11

9

13

3

4 1

8

2

5

A

7

3

1

10

4 2

12

6

5

Wild Rose Star

Wisteria Star

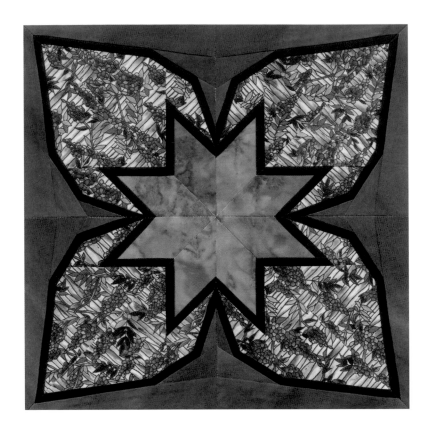

Long dangling tresses of flowers in various shades of lilac, pink, and white make wisteria a favorite ornamental vine. When allowed to run freely, wisteria vines are capable of strangling trees and tearing shingles, gutters, and siding from buildings. Wisteria vines can be trained into a multitude of shapes, but there are two which are especially nice. A single stemmed plant can be trained to grow on a sturdy post. The trunk will become tree-like over time, but must be severely pruned twice a year—first in August and again in early spring. Vines can also be grown on a sturdily built pergola or arbor. This method creates a stunning floral roof each spring providing an unforgettable sight.

Assembly

Make 4 of foundation units A and B. Join the triangles to make a total of 4 squares. Sew the quarters together to make the block.

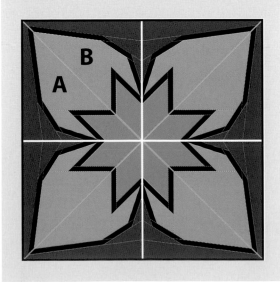

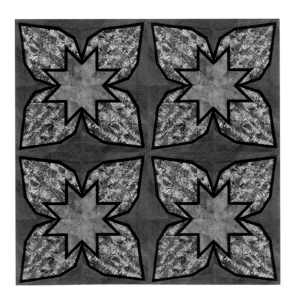

Yardage Requirements (for one block)

⅛ yd. black (leading)
⅛ yd. purple
¼ yd. each green (background) and blue floral

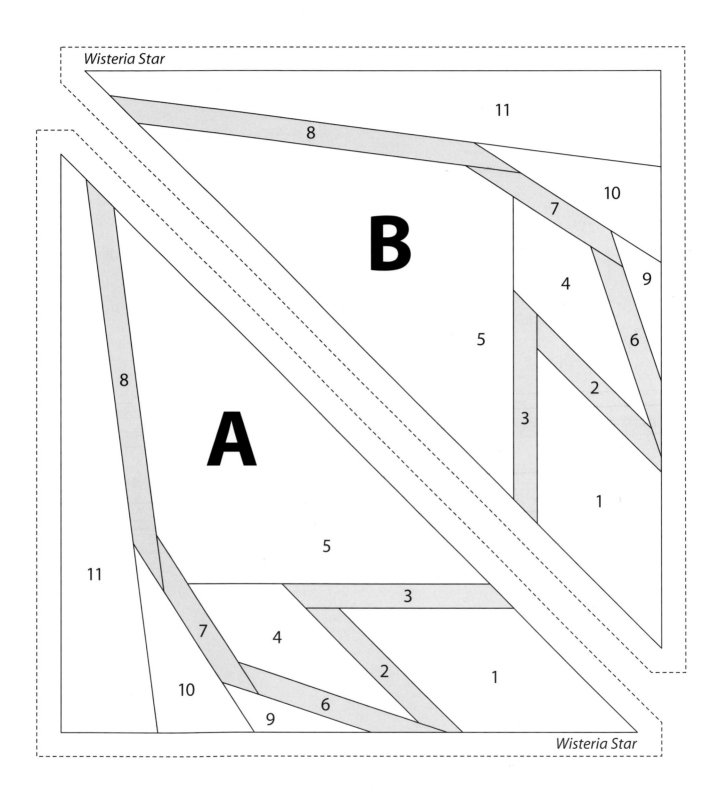

Wisteria Star

Zinnia Star

There are many varieties of zinnias, ranging from dark buttons to tall shaggy cactus flowers. They are available in rich jewel tones of scarlet, ruby and cerise, to orange, gold, primrose, creamy white, and even ice green. At their finest from summer to fall, the season when so many things wilt from the heat, zinnias love the high temperatures, giving so much for so little work. Seeds are sown directly into the ground in the springtime and are very easy to grow. In recent years, small single zinnias have become available that are simply smothered all season long with cheerful 2-inch blossoms. Look for them in your favorite seed catalogs.

Assembly

Make 4 of foundation units A and B. Join the triangles to make a total of 4 squares. Sew the quarters together to make the block.

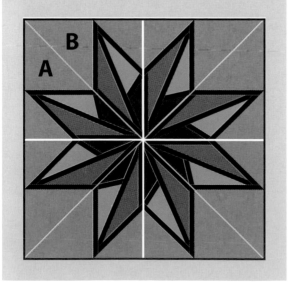

Yardage Requirements (for one block)

⅛ yd. black (leading)
⅛ yd. each orange, violet, and multi-color floral
¼ yd. yellow (background)

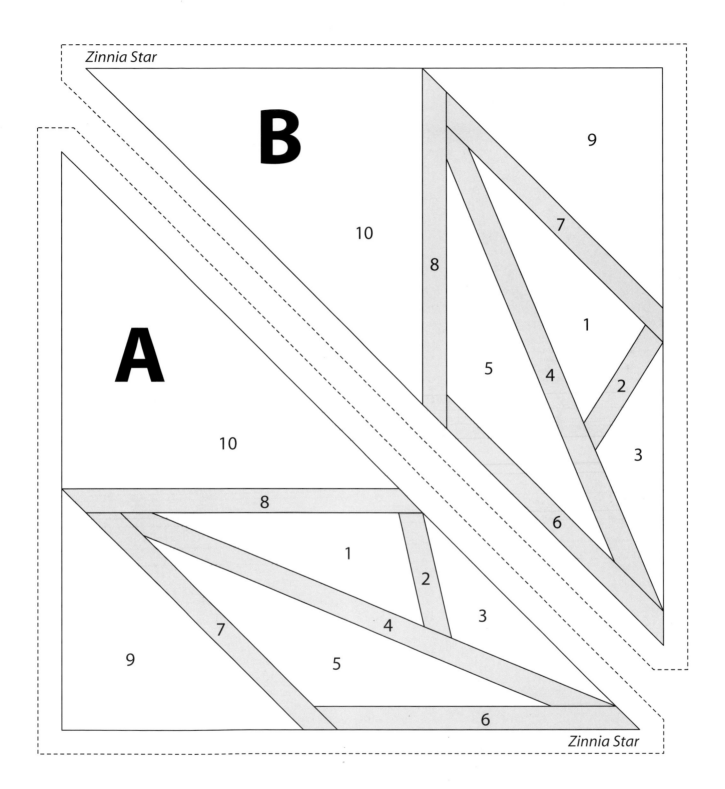

Zinnia Star

B

9

10

7

8

1

5 4 2

3

A

10

8

1

2

7 3

9 4

5 6

Zinnia Star

About the Authors

The iris garden at the bank of Sinking Creek, Newport VA

In 1995, Liz Schwartz and Stephen Seifert cofounded *The Foundation Piecer*, a quilting journal devoted to the art of foundation piecing. In addition to producing books and periodicals, they give lectures and conduct workshops on the foundation piecing technique. They are the authors of five best-selling books: *Birds of a Feather: A gathering of geese, Celestial Wonders: Foundation Pieced Stellar Designs, Foundation Pieced Stained Glass Quilts, The Foundation Piecer: Volume 1,* and *Paper Piecing the Seasons.*

In her spare time, Liz enjoys making flameworked glass beads and Stephen enjoys collecting kaleidoscopes and creating stained glass projects. Both Liz and Stephen live in the Blue Ridge mountains of Virginia with their son, Sebastian.

Resources

Products available from Zippy Designs Publishing

Books
Birds of a Feather: A gathering of Geese
Celestial Wonders: Foundation Pieced Stellar Designs
Foundation Pieced Stained Glass Quilts
Paper Piecing the Seasons
The Foundation Piecer, Volume 1

Periodicals
The Foundation Piecer (quarterly pattern journal)

Tools
Add-a-Quarter Ruler
Easy Piece Foundation Paper
Paper Removal Tweezers
Wooden Seam Pressing Bar

visit us on-line at
www.zippydesigns.com